Building Blocks of C
Learn to Code from Scratch

AUTHOR
Mr. Roger Jees Smith T, M.E(Ph.D)
Assistant Professor, Dept. Of CSE
St. Peter's Engineering College, Hyderabad

ISBN: 979-83-4050-494-4

FIRST EDITION
2024

Copyright ©Roger Jees Smith T Roger Jees Smith T 2024
All rights reserved. The characters and events portrayed in this book are fictitious. Any similarity to real persons, living or dead, is coincidental and not intended by the author.

No part of this book may be reproduced, or stored in a retrieval system, or transmitted in any form or by any means, electronic, mechanical, photocopying, recording, or otherwise, without express written permission of the author.

ISBN-13: 979-83-4050-494-4

Any references to historical events, real people, or real places are used fictitiously. Names, characters, and places are products of the author's imagination

PUBLISHED BY
AMAZON KINDLE DIRECT PUBLISHING
Seattle, Washington, United States
https://kdp.amazon.com

Cover Design, Interior Layout: Author@ Roger Jees Smith T
Printed in the United States of America
Printed on acid-free paper

Preface

Welcome to ***Building Blocks of C-Learn to Code from Scratch***. In a world increasingly defined by technology, programming has become an essential skill, opening doors to diverse opportunities in various fields. This book aims to provide a comprehensive and practical introduction to C programming, aligning with the foundational topics necessary for mastering the language.

The Significance of C Programming

C is often referred to as the "mother of all programming languages." Its influence stretches across countless languages and systems, making it a critical starting point for anyone serious about software development. This guide seeks to demystify C by breaking down complex concepts into manageable, understandable sections. Each topic has been carefully selected to build upon the last, ensuring a coherent learning journey.

Structure of the Book

Our approach is to provide not just theoretical knowledge but practical skills that can be applied immediately. The book is structured as follows:

- **C Introduction**: We begin with an overview of the C programming language, its history, and its role in the evolution of computer science. Understanding the context in which C was developed will help you appreciate its enduring relevance.
- **C Fundamentals**: This section lays the groundwork, introducing the basic syntax and constructs of C. You'll learn about data types, variables, and operators, equipping you with the foundational tools needed for programming.
- **Operators**: We explore the various operators available in C, including arithmetic, relational, and logical operators. Mastery of these will empower you to manipulate data effectively.
- **Control Statements**: This section covers decision-making and looping constructs, such as if-else statements, switch-case constructs, and loops (for, while, do-while). These tools are essential for directing the flow of your programs.
- **Functions**: Functions are the backbone of modular programming. You'll learn how to define and invoke functions, understand scope, and manage return values. This promotes code reusability and clarity.
- **Arrays and Strings**: Here, we delve into data structures that allow you to store collections of data. You'll learn how to declare and manipulate arrays and strings, essential for handling large datasets efficiently.
- **Pointers**: Pointers are a powerful feature of C, enabling you to directly interact with memory. This section will clarify how pointers work, how to use them, and their role in dynamic memory management.

- **Dynamic Memory Allocation (DMA)**: Understanding how to allocate and deallocate memory at runtime is crucial for optimizing resource usage in your applications. We will cover the standard library functions used for DMA, along with best practices.
- **Structures and Unions**: You'll learn how to create complex data types using structures and unions, allowing you to model real-world entities effectively in your programs.
- **Files**: Finally, we explore file handling, equipping you with the skills to read from and write to files. This is vital for data persistence and interacting with external data sources.

Learning Approach

Each chapter contains clear explanations, illustrative examples, and practical exercises designed to reinforce your understanding. The exercises encourage you to apply what you've learned, fostering a hands-on approach that builds confidence and competence.

In addition, we include tips and best practices to help you write clean, efficient code. Throughout your journey, you'll encounter real-world scenarios and challenges that simulate practical programming experiences, preparing you for future endeavors in software development.

For Whom This Book Is Intended

This book is intended for a diverse audience, including students following a curriculum, self-taught learners eager to expand their knowledge, and educators seeking a comprehensive teaching resource. Whether you're just starting out or looking to deepen your understanding of C, this guide offers valuable insights and practical skills.

Conclusion

As you embark on this journey through the world of C programming, we encourage you to embrace curiosity and experimentation. The skills you develop here will serve as a strong foundation for your programming career and will open up a world of possibilities.

Thank you for choosing ***Building Blocks of C-Learn to Code from Scratch***. We hope this book will not only enhance your understanding of C but also inspire you to explore the vast landscape of programming. Let's get started!

Happy coding!

— Roger Jees Smith T

Acknowledgment

Writing *Building Blocks of C-Learn to Code from Scratch* has been an enriching journey, and I am grateful to all those who contributed to its completion.

First and foremost, I would like to thank my family and friends for their unwavering support and encouragement throughout this project. Their patience and belief in my vision kept me motivated during challenging times.

I extend my heartfelt appreciation to my colleagues and fellow educators who provided invaluable insights and feedback. Your expertise and suggestions greatly enhanced the quality of the content and structure of this book. Special thanks to those who reviewed the chapters, offering constructive criticism that helped refine the material.

I am also indebted to the countless programmers and authors whose work has inspired me. Your contributions to the field of computer science have laid the foundation for many learners, including myself.

A special acknowledgment goes to my readers. Your curiosity and determination to learn fuel my passion for teaching and writing. I hope this book serves as a helpful resource on your programming journey.

Finally, I would like to thank the team at [Publisher Name] for their professionalism and support in bringing this book to life. Their expertise in the publishing process ensured that this guide reached its full potential.

Thank you all for being a part of this endeavor. I hope *Building Blocks of C-Learn to Code from Scratch* provides you with the tools and inspiration needed to thrive in your programming pursuits.

— Roger Jees Smith T

Table of Contents

CHAPTER 1: INTRODUCTION TO C _____ **1**
    1.1   C Introduction _____ 1
        1.1.1 History of C _____ 2
        1.1.2 Importance and Applications of C _____ 3
        1.1.3 Features of C _____ 4
        1.1.4 Installation of C _____ 6
        1.1.5 Basic Structure of a C Program _____ 17

CHAPTER 2: C FUNDAMENTALS _____ **26**
    2.1 Token _____ 26
        2.1.1 Keywords _____ 26
        2.1.2 Data Types _____ 27
        2.1.3 Identifier _____ 29
        2.1.4 Variables _____ 30
        2.1.5 Literals _____ 30
        2.1.6 Comments _____ 31
    2.2 Input and Output Functions _____ 33
        2.2.1 scanf() _____ 33
        2.2.2 printf() _____ 34
        2.2.3 Format specifiers _____ 35

CHAPTER 3: OPERATORS _____ **38**
    3.1 Operators _____ 38
        3.1.1 Operators _____ 38
        3.1.2 Operands _____ 38
        3.1.3 Expressions _____ 38
    3.2 Types of Operators in C _____ 40
        3.2.1 Arithmetic Operators _____ 40
        3.2.2 Increment and Decrement Operators _____ 41
        3.2.3 Relational Operators _____ 43
        3.2.4 Assignment Operators _____ 44
        3.2.5 Logical Operators _____ 46
        3.2.6 Bitwise Operators _____ 49
        3.2.7 Conditional (Ternary) Operator _____ 52
        3.2.8 Other Operators _____ 53

CHAPTER 4: CONTROL STATEMENTS _____ **64**
    4.1 Control Statements _____ 64
        4.1.1 Types of Control Statements _____ 64
    4.2 Conditional Statements _____ 64

4.2.1 if statement	65
4.2.2 If-else Statement	66
4.2.3 if-else if or if else ladder	67
4.2.4 nested if else	69
4.2.5 Switch Statement	72
4.2.6 Nested Switch Statement	75
4.3 Loop Statements	79
4.3.1 For Loop	79
4.3.2 While Loop	81
4.3.3 Do-while Loop	86
4.2.4 Nested Loops	89

CHAPTER 5: FUNCTIONS — 92

5.1 Functions Introduction	92
5.1.1 Why Functions	92
5.1.2 Types of Functions in C	94
5.1.3 Parts of a Function in C	94
5.1.4 Function definition and declaration	96
5.1.5 Function Arguments and Return Values	98
5.1.6 Scope and Lifetime of Variables	99
5.1.7 Types of Variables	101
5.1.8 Recursive Functions	102
5.1.9 Inline Functions	105
5.1.10 Storage Classes	106

CHAPTER 6: ARRAYS — 110

6.1 Arrays	110
6.1.1 Arrays Introduction	110
6.1.2 Why Use Arrays in C	110
6.2 Types of Arrays in C	112
6.2.1 One-Dimensional Arrays	112
6.2.2 Two-Dimensional Arrays	116
6.2.3 Multi-Dimensional Arrays	119

CHAPTER 7: STRINGS — 123

7.1 Strings Introduction	123
7.1.1 Strings Declaration	123
7.1.2 Strings Initialization	124
7.1.3 Reading Strings from Keyboard	124
7.2 String Buit-in Functions	126

CHAPTER 8: STRUCTURES AND UNIONS — 132

8.1 Structure	132
8.1.2 Creating Structure	133
8.1.3 Memory allocation of Structure	136
8.2 Union	137

8.2.1 Union Declaration _____ 138
8.2.2 Accessing the Union Members _____ 139
8.2.3 Initialization of Union Members _____ 140
8.2.4 Size and memory allocation of Union _____ 141
8.2.5 Difference between Structure and Union _____ 147
8.3 Typedef and Enumerations _____ 147

CHAPTER 9: POINTERS _____ 149

9.1 Pointer Introduction _____ 150
   9.1.1 Pointers Arithmetic Operations in C _____ 155
   9.1.2 Pointers to Pointers in C _____ 158
   9.1.3 Pointers to Arrays in C _____ 159
   9.1.4 Pointers for Functions in C _____ 161
9.2 Dynamic Memory Allocation _____ 163

CHAPTER 10: PREPROCESSORS AND MACROS _____ 172

10.1 Proprocessors Introduction _____ 172
10.2 Types of C Preprocessors _____ 173
   10.2.1 Macros _____ 174
   10.2.2 File Include Directive _____ 176
   10.2.3 Conditional Compilation _____ 179

Exercise Programs _____ 182

CHAPTER 1: INTRODUCTION TO C

1.1 C Introduction
C programming is a high-level programming language that provides a powerful set of features for system and application development. some key aspects:
1. *General Purpose:* C is a general-purpose language, meaning it can be used to write software for a wide variety of applications, from operating systems and embedded systems to applications and games.
2. *Procedural Language:* C follows a procedural programming paradigm, emphasizing functions and procedures for organizing code and solving problems.
3. *Efficiency:* C is known for its performance and efficiency, allowing developers to write fast and resource-efficient code. This is especially important in systems programming and resource-constrained environments.
4. *Low-Level Access:* C provides low-level access to memory through the use of pointers, enabling fine control over hardware and system resources.
5. *Portability:* Programs written in C can be compiled and run on various hardware and operating systems with minimal changes, making it highly portable.
6. *Rich Set of Libraries:* C has a rich set of standard libraries that provide pre-built functions for various tasks, such as string manipulation, mathematical computations, and file I/O.
7. *Wide Adoption:* C is widely used in software development, including operating systems (like UNIX and Linux), embedded systems, database systems, and application development.

C programming is a foundational language that has influenced many modern programming languages. Its efficiency, control, and flexibility make it a popular choice for both beginners and experienced developers in various fields of software development.

C programming is considered as the base for other programming languages, that is why it is known as the mother language.

It can be defined by the following ways:
1. Mother language
2. System programming language
3. Procedure-oriented programming language
4. Structured programming language
5. Mid-level programming language

1) C as a mother language
C language is considered as the mother language of all modern programming languages because most of the compilers, JVMs, Kernels, etc. are written in C

language, and most of the programming languages follow C syntax, for example, C++, Java, C#, etc.

It provides the core concepts like the array, strings, functions, file handling, etc. that are being used in many languages like C++, Java, C#, etc.

2) C as a system programming language

A system programming language is used to create system software. C language is a system programming language because it can be used to do low-level programming (for example driver and kernel). It is generally used to create hardware devices, OS, drivers, kernels, etc. For example, Linux kernel is written in C.It can't be used for internet programming like Java, .Net, PHP, etc.

3) C as a procedural language

A procedure is known as a function, method, routine, subroutine, etc. A procedural language specifies a series of steps for the program to solve the problem.

A procedural language breaks the program into functions, data structures, etc.

C is a procedural language. In C, variables and function prototypes must be declared before being used.

4) C as a structured programming language

A structured programming language is a subset of the procedural language. Structure means to break a program into parts or blocks so that it may be easy to understand.

In the C language, we break the program into parts using functions. It makes the program easier to understand and modify.

5) C as a mid-level programming language

C is considered as a middle-level language because it supports the feature of both low-level and high-level languages. C language program is converted into assembly code, it supports pointer arithmetic (low-level), but it is machine independent (a feature of high-level).

A Low-level language is specific to one machine, i.e., machine dependent. It is machine dependent, fast to run. But it is not easy to understand.

A High-Level language is not specific to one machine, i.e., machine independent. It is easy to understand.

1.1.1 History of C

C programming language was developed in 1972 by Dennis Ritchie at bell laboratories of AT&T (American Telephone & Telegraph), located in the U.S.A. Dennis Ritchie is known as the founder of the c language.

It was developed to overcome the problems of previous languages such as B, BCPL, etc.

Initially, C language was developed to be used in UNIX operating system. It inherits many features of previous languages such as B and BCPL.

Let's see the programming languages that were developed before C language.

Language	Year	Developed By
Algol	1960	International Group
BCPL	1967	Martin Richard
B	1970	Ken Thompson
Traditional C	1972	Dennis Ritchie
K & R C	1978	Kernighan & Dennis Ritchie
ANSI C	1989	ANSI Committee
ANSI/ISO C	1990	ISO Committee
C99	1999	Standardization Committee

1.1.2 Importance and Applications of C

C programming holds significant importance in the field of computer science and software development for several reasons:

1. Foundation for Other Languages
- *Influence on Modern Languages:* Many programming languages, including C++, Java, and Python, draw syntax and concepts from C. Understanding C provides a solid foundation for learning these languages.
- *Object-Oriented Programming:* C++ was developed as an extension of C, introducing object-oriented features while retaining C's procedural nature.

2. Efficiency and Performance
- *Low-Level Access:* C allows direct manipulation of hardware through pointers, enabling high-performance applications, especially in system programming and embedded systems.
- *Speed:* Programs written in C are often faster and more efficient than those written in higher-level languages, making it ideal for performance-critical applications.

3. Portability
- *Cross-Platform Development:* C code can be compiled on various platforms with minimal changes, enhancing its portability. This is crucial for developing software that runs on different operating systems.

4. System Programming
- *Operating Systems:* C is widely used in the development of operating systems (e.g., UNIX, Linux) and system-level software due to its ability to interact closely with hardware.
- **Embedded Systems**: Many embedded systems are programmed in C, as it allows for efficient use of limited resources.

5. Modularity and Reusability
- *Functions and Libraries:* C promotes modular programming through functions, allowing developers to write reusable code and improve

maintainability. Standard libraries provide pre-built functions that enhance productivity.

6. Understanding Computer Science Concepts
- *Memory Management:* C requires explicit memory management, helping programmers understand concepts like memory allocation, pointers, and data structures, which are vital in computer science.
- *Data Structures:* Learning C helps in mastering data structures such as arrays, linked lists, trees, and graphs, which are essential for algorithm development.

7. Widely Used in Academia and Industry
- *Educational Tool:* C is often taught in computer science curricula as a first programming language, as it covers fundamental programming concepts and problem-solving skills.
- *Industry Demand:* Many organizations seek developers with C programming skills, especially in sectors like systems programming, game development, and embedded systems.

8. Community and Resources
- *Rich Ecosystem:* C has a large community of developers and extensive resources available, including libraries, frameworks, and online courses, making it easier for learners to find support.

C programming is vital for understanding computing principles and developing efficient software. Its widespread use in both industry and education, combined with its performance and portability, solidifies its importance in the programming landscape.

1.1.3 Features of C
C is the widely used language. It provides many features that are given below.

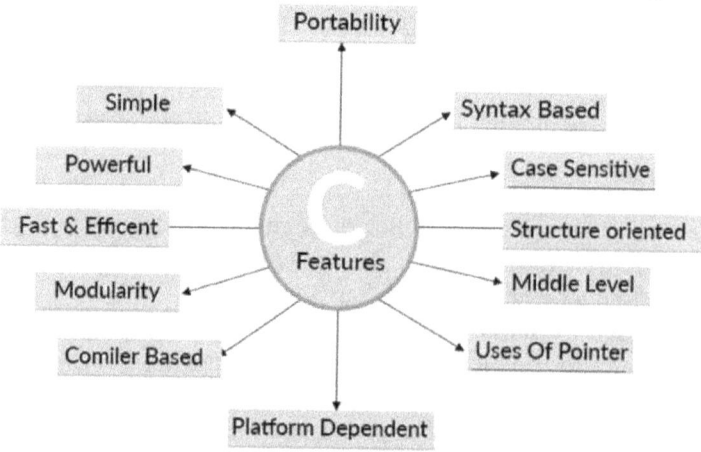

1. Simple
2. Machine Independent or Portable

3. Mid-level programming language
4. structured programming language
5. Rich Library
6. Memory Management
7. Fast Speed
8. Pointers
9. Recursion
10. Extensible

1) Simple
C is a simple language in the sense that it provides a structured approach (to break the problem into parts), the rich set of library functions, data types, etc.

2) Machine Independent or Portable
Unlike assembly language, c programs can be executed on different machines with some machine specific changes. Therefore, C is a machine independent language.

3) Mid-level programming language
Although, C is intended to do low-level programming. It is used to develop system applications such as kernel, driver, etc. It also supports the features of a high-level language. That is why it is known as mid-level language.

4) Structured programming language
C is a structured programming language in the sense that we can break the program into parts using functions. So, it is easy to understand and modify. Functions also provide code reusability.

5) Rich Library
C provides a lot of inbuilt functions that make the development fast.

6) Memory Management
It supports the feature of dynamic memory allocation. In C language, we can free the allocated memory at any time by calling the free() function.

7) Speed
The compilation and execution time of C language is fast since there are lesser inbuilt functions and hence the lesser overhead.

8) Pointer
C provides the feature of pointers. We can directly interact with the memory by using the pointers. We can use pointers for memory, structures, functions, array, etc.

9) Recursion
In C, we can call the function within the function. It provides code reusability for every function. Recursion enables us to use the approach of backtracking.

10) Extensible
C language is extensible because it can easily adopt new features.

1.1.4 Installation of C
To execute C programs, you need a combination of tools and software that includes a code editor, a compiler, and an integrated development environment (IDE).

Text Editors

These are used to write the source code. Some popular text editors include:
- Notepad++ (Windows)
- Sublime Text (Cross-platform)
- Visual Studio Code (Cross-platform)
- Vim (Cross-platform)
- Emacs (Cross-platform)
- Atom (Cross-platform)

Compilers

A compiler translates the C source code into machine code that can be executed by the computer. Some commonly used C compilers are:

GCC (GNU Compiler Collection):
A widely-used open-source compiler that supports various programming languages, including C.
Available on Linux, Windows (via MinGW or Cygwin), and macOS.

Clang:
A compiler that is part of the LLVM project, known for its fast compilation and useful diagnostics. Available on Linux, Windows, and macOS.

Microsoft Visual C++ (MSVC):
Part of Microsoft Visual Studio, a robust IDE that includes a compiler for C and C++.

Turbo C and Turbo C++:
An older compiler, once popular in educational environments.
Available on Windows (mostly used for legacy purposes).

Integrated Development Environments (IDEs) for C Programs
- Code::Blocks
- Dev-C++
- Eclipse CDT (C/C++ Development Tooling)
- Microsoft Visual Studio
- Xcode
- NetBeans

Online Compilers for C Programs

For quick testing and small projects, online compilers can be very convenient. Some popular online compilers include:
- OnlineGDB: https://www.onlinegdb.com/
- Repl.it: https://replit.com/
- JDoodle: https://www.jdoodle.com/
- Compiler Explorer: https://godbolt.org/

Installation of Turbo C++:
Turbo C++:
It will work for both C and C++. To install the Turbo C++ software, you need to follow following steps.
1. Download Turbo C++
2. Create turboc directory inside c drive and extract the tc3.zip inside c:\turboc
3. Double click on install.exe file
4. Click on the tc application file located inside c:\TC\BIN to write the c program

1) Download Turbo C++ software
You can download turbo c++ from many sites. download Turbo c++
2) Create turboc directory in c drive and extract the tc3.zip
Now, you need to create a new directory turboc inside the c: drive. Now extract the tc3.zip file in c:\truboc directory.
3) Double click on the install.exe file and follow steps
Now, click on the install icon located inside the c:\turboc

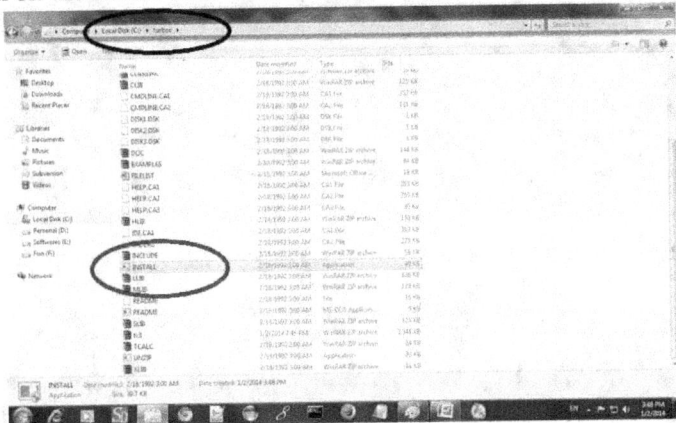

It will ask you to install c or not, press enter to install.

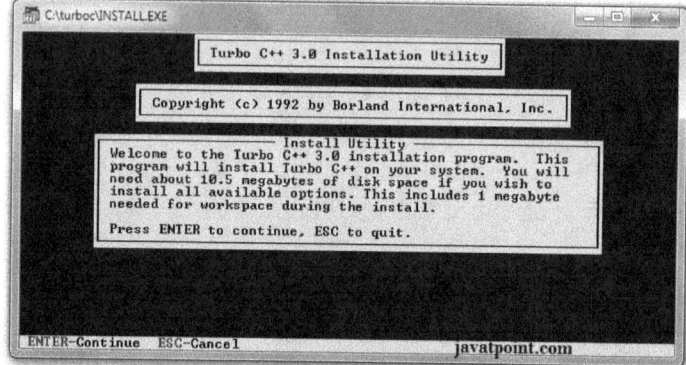

Change your drive to c, press c.

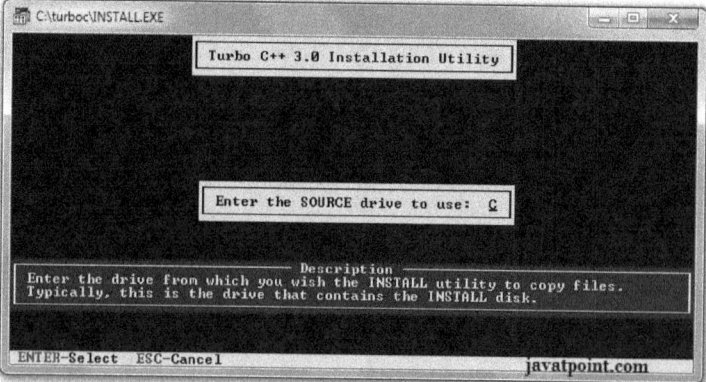

Press enter, it will look inside the c:\turboc directory for the required files.

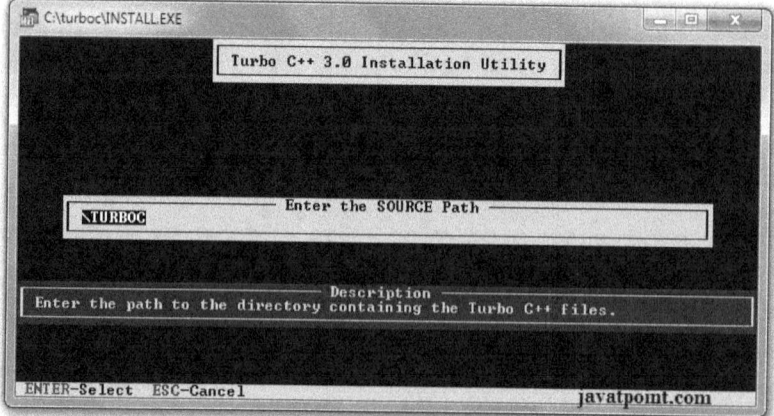

Select Start installation by the down arrow key then press enter.

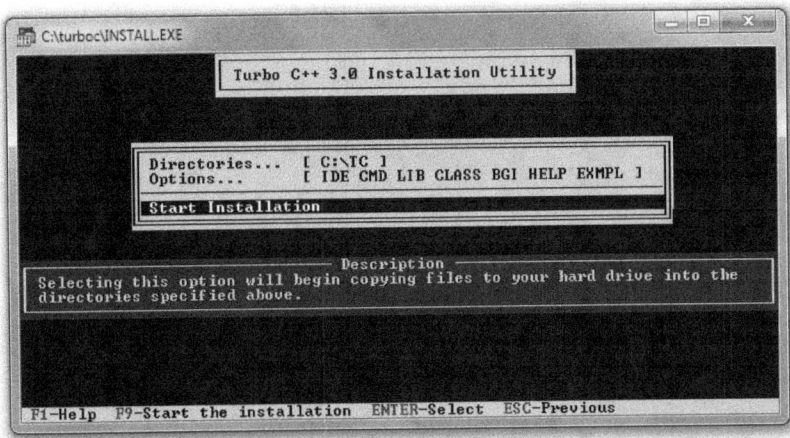

Now C is installed, press enter to read documentation or close the software.

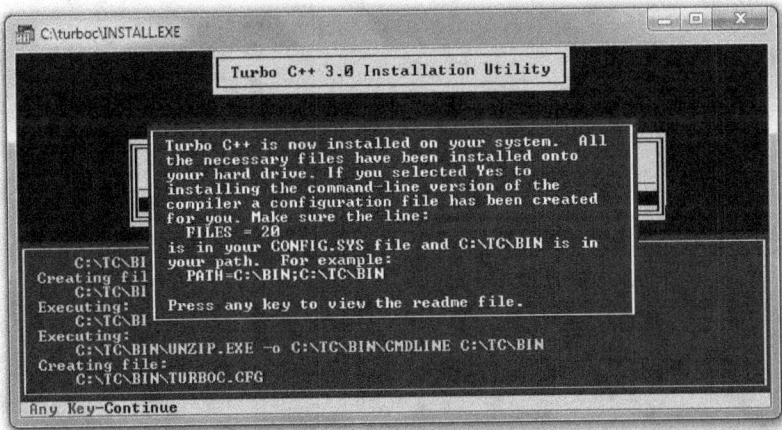

4) Click on the tc application located inside c:\TC\BIN

Now double click on the tc icon located in c:\TC\BIN directory to write the c program.

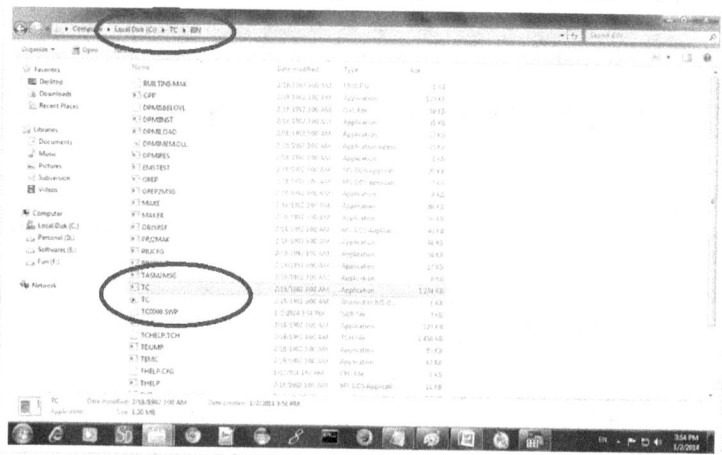

In windows 7 or window 8, it will show a dialog block to ignore and close the application because fullscreen mode is not supported. Click on Ignore button. Now it will showing following console.

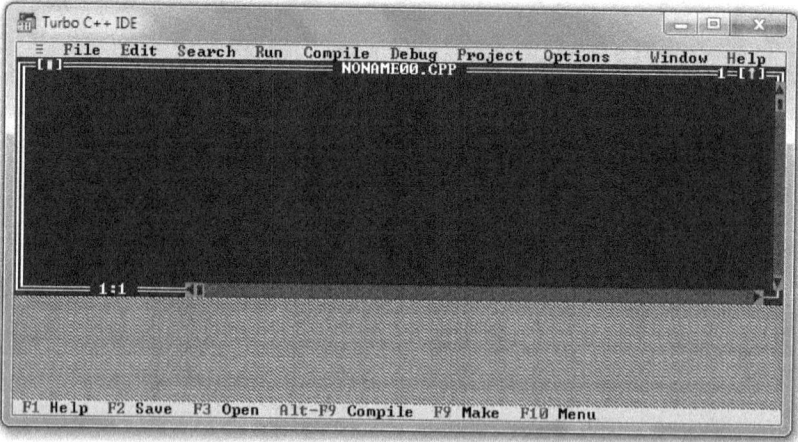

Installation of Dev C++:
To download and install Dev-C++, follow these steps:
Step 1: Download Dev-C++
1. **Visit the Official Site**: Go to the official Dev-C++ website or a trusted source, such as Bloodshed's Dev-C++ or Orwel's Dev-C++.
2. **Download the Installer**: Look for the download link for the latest version and click on it. You'll typically get an .exe file.

Step 2: Install Dev-C++
1. **Run the Installer**: Locate the downloaded .exe file and double-click it to start the installation.
2. **Choose Installation Options**: Follow the on-screen instructions:

- Accept the license agreement.
- Choose the installation directory (the default is usually fine).
- Select components to install (if prompted).

3. **Complete Installation**: Click "Install" and wait for the process to finish. Then, click "Finish" to exit the installer.

Step 3: Launch Dev-C++
1. **Open Dev-C++**: You can find it in your Start Menu or on your desktop.
2. **Configure (if necessary)**: The first time you run it, you may want to configure the settings according to your preferences.

Step 4: Create a New Project
1. **Start a New Project**: Go to File > New > Project to begin coding.
2. **Choose Project Type**: Select a console application (for C/C++) and give your project a name.

Step 5: Write and Compile Code
1. **Write Your Code**: Use the editor to write your C or C++ code.
2. **Compile**: Click on Execute > Compile & Run or press F9 to compile and run your program.

Tips
- Ensure you have the necessary permissions to install software on your machine.
- If you encounter issues, check if you have the required C/C++ compilers set up correctly.

The following Screenshots show the download and installation of Dev C++

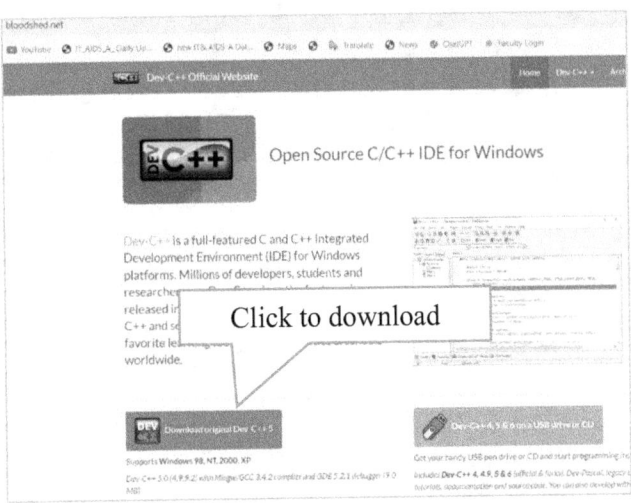

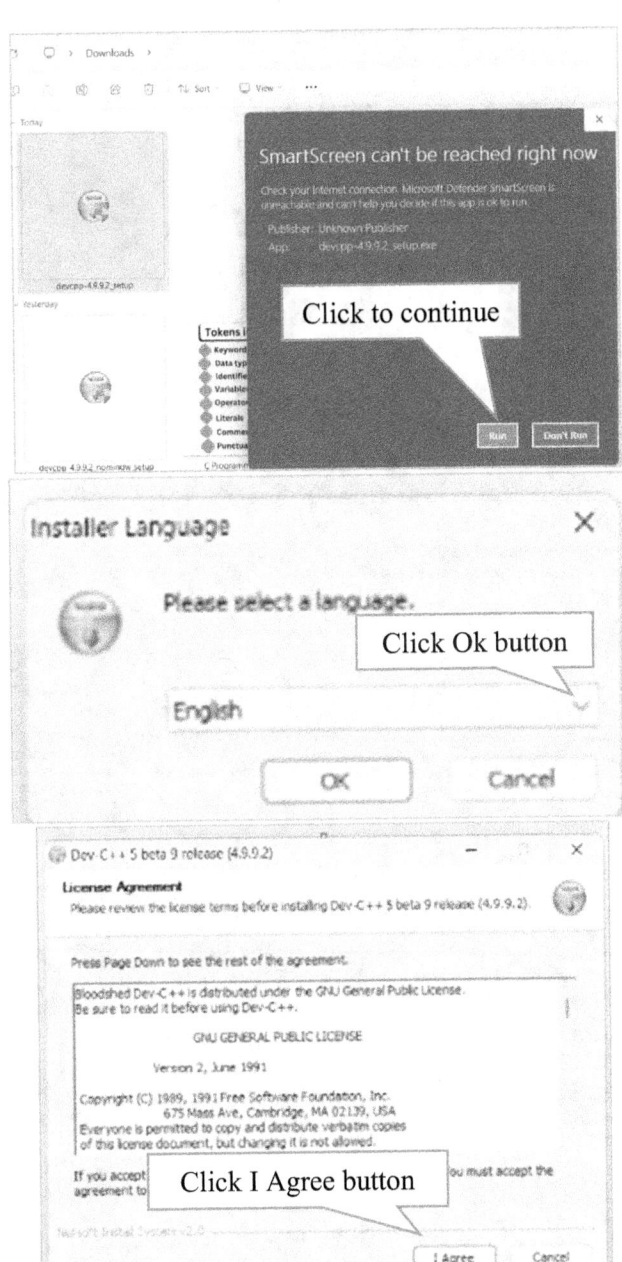

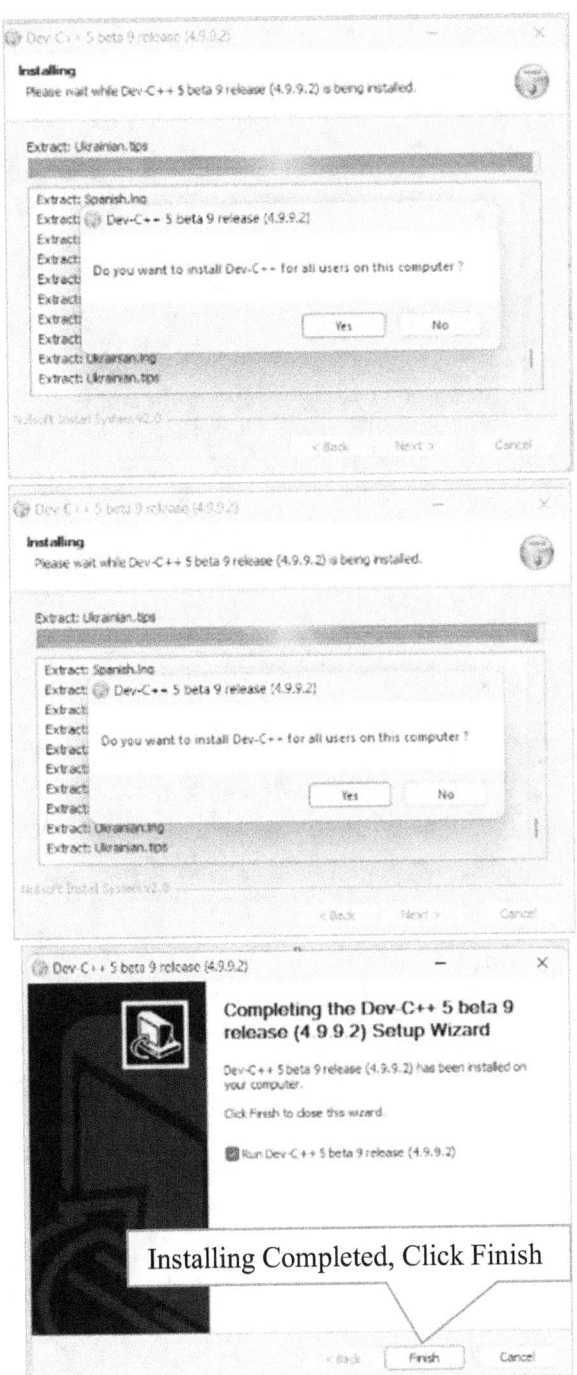

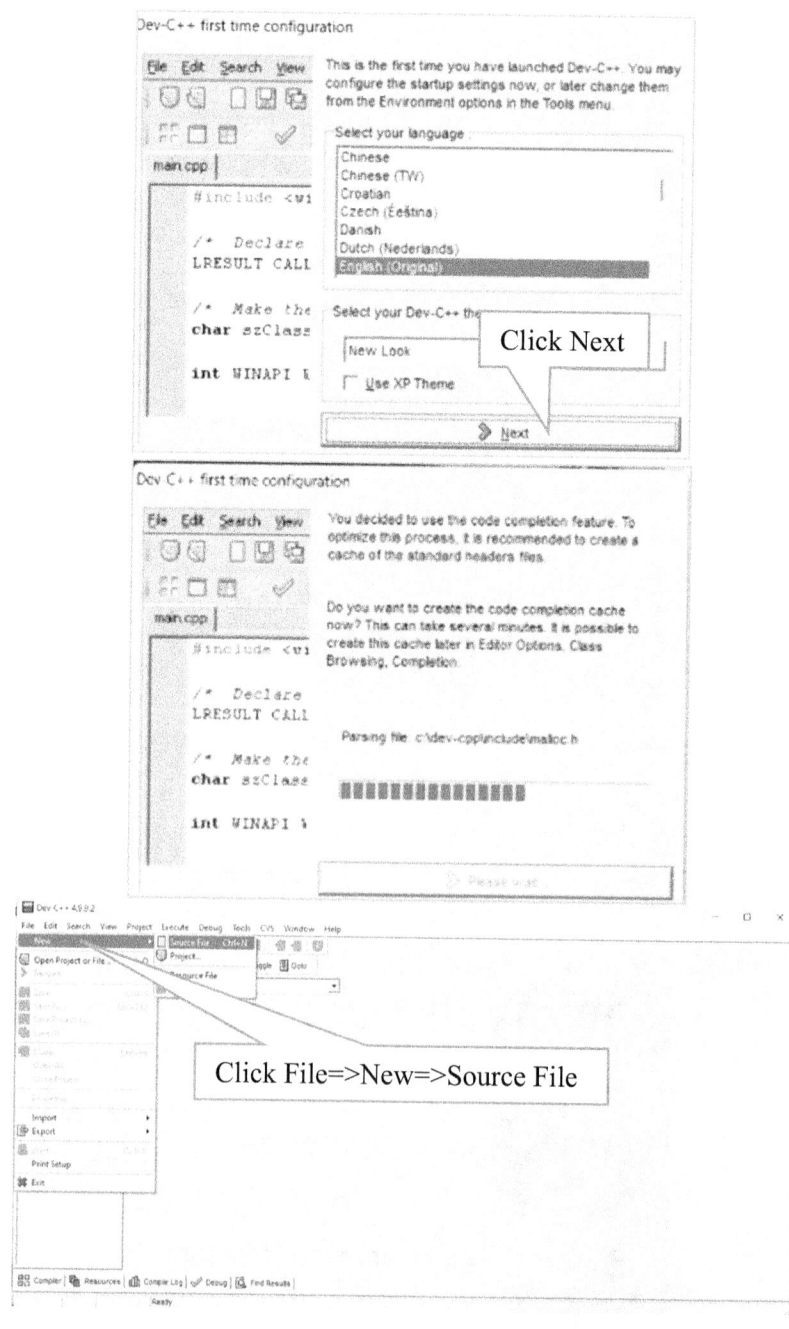

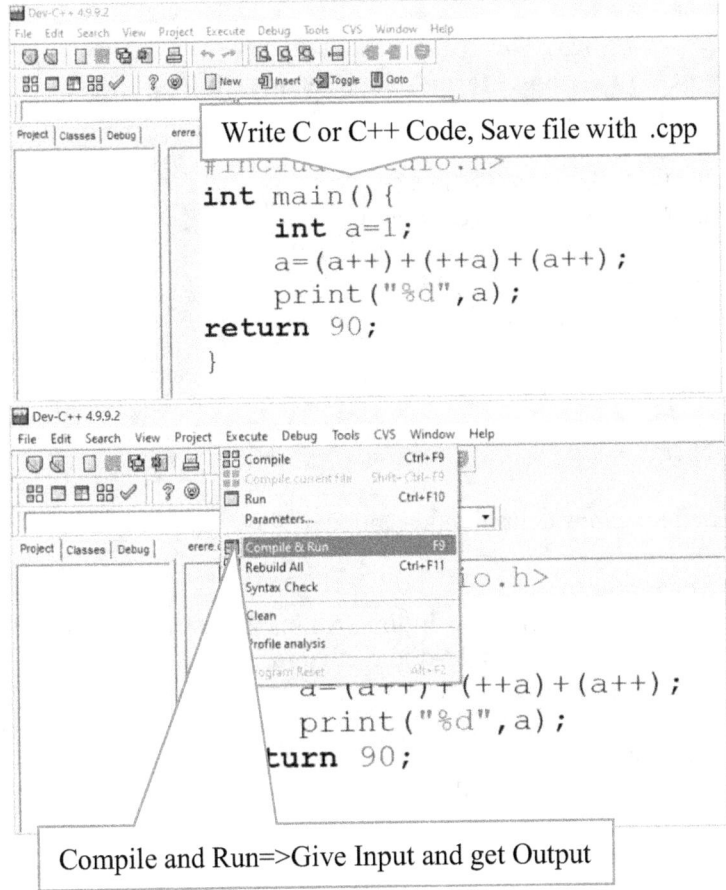

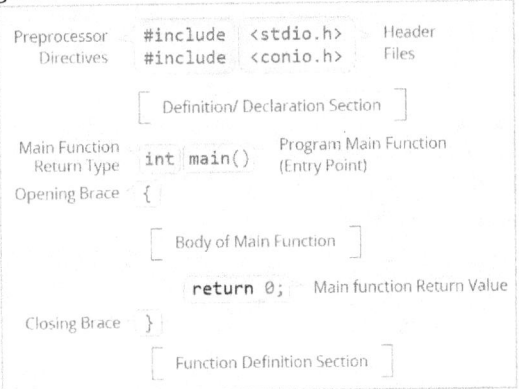

1.1.5 Basic Structure of a C Program
The syntax of a basic C program follows a specific structure and order as below
Syntax of C Program

Structure of C Program in terms of statements wise:
Preprocessor Directives
    Header Files inclusion
    Constants Declaration (Optional)
Global Variables Declaration (Optional)
User-Defined function(s) Prototype (Optional)
Int or Void   main(Arguments-Optional) {
  Local Variable Declaration
  Read the input
  Main Logic/Statements or Function calls
  Print the output
  Return statement
}
User-defined functions definition(s)-Optional

Sample C Program
```c
#include <stdio.h>   // Preprocessor directive for standard input-output
#include <math.h>    // Preprocessor directive for math functions
#define PI 3.14159   // Define a constant

// Function prototype
double calculateArea(double radius);

// Global variable
int globalCount = 0;

int main() {
    // Local variable declarations
    double radius, area;

    // Input from user
    printf("Enter the radius of the circle: ");
    scanf("%lf", &radius);

    // Function call
    area = calculateArea(radius);

    // Output the result
    printf("The area of the circle with radius %.2f is %.2f\n", radius, area);

    // Increment and print global variable
```

```
    globalCount++;
    printf("Global count: %d\n", globalCount);

    return 0;
}

// Function definition
double calculateArea(double radius) {
    return PI * radius * radius;  // Calculate area using the formula
}
```

About Each Section of a Program

- **Preprocessor section**

The preprocessor section contains all the header files used in a program. It informs the system to link the header files to the system libraries. It is given by:
1. #include<stdio.h>
2. #include<conio.h>

The #include statement includes the specific file as a part of a function at the time of the compilation. Thus, the contents of the included file are compiled along with the function being compiled. The #include<stdio.h> consists of the contents of the standard input output files, which contain the definition of stdin, stdout, and stderr. Whenever the definitions stdin, stdout, and stderr are used in a function, the statement #include<stdio.h> need to be used.

- **Define section**

The define section comprises of different constants declared using the define keyword. It is given by:
1. #define a = 2

- **Global declaration**

The global section comprises of all the global declarations in the program. It is given by:
1. float num = 2.54;
2. int a = 5;
3. char ch ='z';

The size of the above global variables is listed as follows:
    char = 1 byte
    float = 4 bytes
    int = 4 bytes

We can also declare user defined functions in the global variable section.

- **Main function**

main() is the first function to be executed by the computer. It is necessary for a code to include the main(). It is like any other function available in the C library. Parenthesis () are used for passing parameters (if any) to a function.
The main function is declared as:

         main()
We can also use int or main with the main (). The void main() specifies that the program will not return any value. The int main() specifies that the program can return integer type data.
         int main()
Or
         void main()
Main function is further categorized into local declarations, statements, and expressions.
- **Local declarations**

The variable that is declared inside a given function or block refers to as local declarations.
         main()
         {
         int i = 2;
         i++;
         }
- **Statements**

The statements refers to if, else, while, do, for, etc. used in a program within the main function.
- **Expressions**

An expression is a type of formula where operands are linked with each other by the use of operators. It is given by:
         a - b;
         a +b;
- **User defined functions**

The user defined functions specified the functions specified as per the requirements of the user. For example, color(), sum(), division(), etc.
The program (basic or advance) follows the same sections as listed above.
- **Return Statement**

Return statement is generally the last section of a code. But, it is not necessary to include. It is used when we want to return a value. The return function returns a value when the return type other than the void is specified with the function.
Return type ends the execution of the function. It further returns control to the specified calling function. It is given by:
         return;
Or
         return expression ;
For example,
return 0;
Let's begin with a simple program in C language.
Example 1: To find the sum of two numbers given by the user

It is given by:

```
/* Sum of two numbers */
#include<stdio.h>
int main()
{
int a, b, sum;
printf("Enter two numbers to be added ");
 scanf("%d %d", &a, &b);
 // calculating sum
 sum = a + b;
 printf("%d + %d = %d", a, b, sum);
 return 0; // return the integer value in the sum
}
```

Output

```
Enter two numbers to be added 3 5
3 + 5 = 8
```

The detailed explanation of each part of a code is as follows:

* Sum of the two numbers */	It is the comment section. Any statement described in it is not considered as a code. It is a part of the description section in a code. The comment line is optional. It can be in a separate line or part of an executable line.
#include<stdio.h>	It is the standard input-output header file. It is a command of the preprocessor section.
int main()	main() is the first function to be executed in every program. We have used int with the main() in order to return an integer value.
{... }	The curly braces mark the beginning and end of a function. It is mandatory in all the functions.
printf()	The printf() prints text on the screen. It is a function for displaying constant or variables data. Here, 'Enter two

	numbers to be added' is the parameter passed to it.
scanf()	It reads data from the standard input stream and writes the result into the specified arguments.
sum = a + b	The addition of the specified two numbers will be passed to the sum parameter in the output.
return 0	A program can also run without a return 0 function. It simply states that a program is free from error and can be successfully exited.

Example program
1.Write a C Program to display "Hello World"
#include <stdio.h>

int main() {
   printf("Hello, World!\n");
   return 0;
}
Output:
Hello, World!
2.Write a C Program to display Your name 5 times.
#include <stdio.h>

int main() {
   // Replace "Your Name" with your actual name
   const char *name = "Your Name";

   printf("%s\n", name);
   printf("%s\n", name);
   printf("%s\n", name);
   printf("%s\n", name);
   printf("%s\n", name);

   return 0;
}
Output:

Your Name
Your Name
Your Name
Your Name
Your Name

3. Write a C Program to read the values from keyboard and print.

```c
#include <stdio.h>

int main() {
    int value; // Variable to hold the integer value

    // Prompt the user for input
    printf("Enter an integer: ");
    scanf("%d", &value); // Read an integer from the keyboard

    // Print the value
    printf("You entered: %d\n", value);

    return 0;
}
```

Output:
Enter an integer: 25
You entered: 25

4. Write a C Program to read the value into every data type of C supported and print the values.

```c
#include <stdio.h>

int main() {
    int integerValue;
    float floatValue;
    double doubleValue;
    char charValue;
    char stringValue[100]; // Array to hold a string

    // Read values from the keyboard
    printf("Enter an integer: ");
    scanf("%d", &integerValue);

    printf("Enter a float: ");
    scanf("%f", &floatValue);

    printf("Enter a double: ");
    scanf("%lf", &doubleValue);
```

```c
    printf("Enter a character: ");
    scanf(" %c", &charValue); // Note the space before %c to consume any leftover newline

    printf("Enter a string: ");
    scanf("%s", stringValue); // Read a string (single word)

    // Print the values
    printf("\nYou entered:\n");
    printf("Integer: %d\n", integerValue);
    printf("Float: %.2f\n", floatValue);
    printf("Double: %.2lf\n", doubleValue);
    printf("Character: %c\n", charValue);
    printf("String: %s\n", stringValue);

    return 0;
}
```
Output:
Enter an integer: 42
Enter a float: 3.14
Enter a double: 2.7182818284
Enter a character: A
Enter a string: Hello

You entered:
Integer: 42
Float: 3.14
Double: 2.72
Character: A
String: Hello

5. Write a C Program to read two numbers add them and display their sum.

```c
#include <stdio.h>

int main() {
    // Declare variables to hold the two numbers and their sum
    float num1, num2, sum;

    // Prompt the user for input
    printf("Enter the first number: ");
    scanf("%f", &num1); // Read the first number
```

```c
    printf("Enter the second number: ");
    scanf("%f", &num2); // Read the second number

    // Calculate the sum
    sum = num1 + num2;

    // Display the result
    printf("The sum of %.2f and %.2f is %.2f\n", num1, num2, sum);

    return 0;
}
```
Output:
Enter the first number: 10.5
Enter the second number: 5.75
The sum of 10.50 and 5.75 is 16.25

CHAPTER 2: C FUNDAMENTALS

2.1 Token

A token is the smallest element of a program that is meaningful to the compiler. The compiler breaks the source code into tokens, which it then uses to understand and translate the program into machine code. Tokens are the building blocks of a C program.

Tokens in C
- Keywords
- Data types
- Identifiers
- Variables
- Operators
- Literals
- Comments
- Punctuation (Separators)

2.1.1 Keywords

A keyword is a special reserved word that has a specific meaning and purpose in the language. Keywords cannot be used as identifiers (variable names, function names, etc.) because they are already defined by the C language for a specific purpose.

Keywords in C Programming			
auto	break	case	char
const	continue	default	do
double	else	enum	extern
float	for	goto	if
int	long	register	return
short	signed	sizeof	static

Keywords in C Programming			
struct	switch	typedef	union
unsigned	void	volatile	while

2.1.2 Data Types

A data type specifies the type of data that a variable can store such as integer, floating, character, etc. In C programming, data types are declarations for variables. This determines the type and size of data associated with variables.

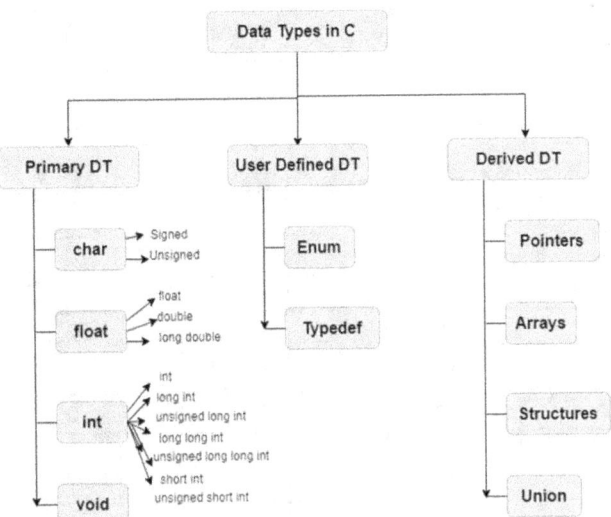

Primary Datatypes

In C, primary data types (often referred to as basic or fundamental data types) are the most basic types of data that can be used to define variables. They are built into the language and form the foundation for data manipulation.

- **int**: Whole numbers (e.g., int count;)
- **float**: Single-precision decimals (e.g., float price;)
- **double**: Double-precision decimals (e.g., double distance;)
- **char**: Single characters (e.g., char initial;)

These data types allow you to create variables that can store numerical values, characters, and other data, serving as the building blocks for more complex data structures. The Size of each data type occupied in computer memory and format specifier is used to each data type as given in two tables are:

Type	Size (bytes)	Format Specifier
int	at least 2, usually 4	%d, %i
char	1	%c
float	4	%f
double	8	%lf
short int	2 usually	%hd
unsigned int	at least 2, usually 4	%u
long int	at least 4, usually 8	%ld, %li
long long int	at least 8	%lld, %lli
unsigned long int	at least 4	%lu
unsigned long long int	at least 8	%llu
signed char	1	%c
unsigned char	1	%c
long double	at least 10, usually 12 or 16	%Lf

Data Types	Memory Size	Range
char	1 byte	−128 to 127
signed char	1 byte	−128 to 127
unsigned char	1 byte	0 to 255
short	2 byte	−32,768 to 32,767
signed short	2 byte	−32,768 to 32,767
unsigned short	2 byte	0 to 65,535
int	2 byte	−32,768 to 32,767
signed int	2 byte	−32,768 to 32,767
unsigned int	2 byte	0 to 65,535
short int	2 byte	−32,768 to 32,767
signed short int	2 byte	−32,768 to 32,767
unsigned short int	2 byte	0 to 65,535
long int	4 byte	-2,147,483,648 to 2,147,483,647
signed long int	4 byte	-2,147,483,648 to 2,147,483,647
unsigned long int	4 byte	0 to 4,294,967,295
float	4 byte	
double	8 byte	
long double	10 byte	

Derived data types
Derived data types in C are types that are constructed from the basic data types. They allow you to create more complex data structures that can hold multiple values or different types of data.
- **Arrays**: Collections of similar data types.
- **Structures**: Grouping of different data types.
- **Unions**: Storage for different types in the same memory location.
- **Function Pointers**: Pointers that point to functions.

Derived data types provide flexibility and allow for the creation of complex data structures, making it easier to manage and manipulate related data in C programs

User-defined data type
In C, a user-defined data type is a data type that is defined by the programmer rather than provided by the language itself. This allows for more complex and structured data management tailored to specific needs.
- **Enumerations (enum)**: Named constants for clarity.
- **Typedef**: Creating aliases for existing types for better readability.

User-defined data types enable programmers to create complex data models that fit the needs of their applications, making the code more organized and maintainable

2.1.3 Identifier
In C, an **identifier** is a name used to identify a variable, function, array, structure, or any other user-defined item. Identifiers are essential for naming and accessing these elements in your code.

Rules for Identifiers
1. **Allowed Characters**: Identifiers can consist of letters (both uppercase and lowercase), digits (0-9), and underscores (_). However, they cannot start with a digit.
2. **Case Sensitivity**: Identifiers are case-sensitive, meaning myVariable and myvariable are different identifiers.
3. **Length**: There is no strict limit on the length of identifiers, but it's good practice to keep them reasonably short and descriptive.
4. **Reserved Keywords**: Identifiers cannot be the same as C keywords (like int, return, etc.).

Examples of Valid Identifiers
- count: A simple identifier.
- totalSum: A valid identifier with mixed case.
- _index: Starts with an underscore, which is allowed.
- userName1: Combines letters and digits.

Examples of Invalid Identifiers
- 1stValue: Starts with a digit, which is not allowed.
- total sum: Contains a space, which is not permitted.
- int: A reserved keyword, cannot be used as an identifier.

2.1.4 Variables
In C programming, a variable is a name given to a memory location that is used to store data or value. Variables are used to hold values that can be change during the program execution. Each variable has a unique name (also called an identifier) used to reference its value.
Characteristics of Variables
Type:
Each variable has a type that defines the kind of data it can store. The type determines the size and layout of the variable's memory, the range of values it can hold, and the operations that can be performed on it. Common types include:
int: Integer numbers (e.g., int age = 25;)
float and double: Floating-point numbers (e.g., float temperature = 23.5;)
char: Single characters (e.g., char initial = 'A';)
void: Represents the absence of type.
Score:
The scope of a variable determines the context in which it is accessible. There are several types of scope in C:
Local scope: Variables declared inside a function or block are local to that function or block.
Global scope: Variables declared outside all functions are global and can be accessed from any function within the same file.
Static scope: Static variables retain their value between function calls and can have either local or global scope.
Lifetime:
The lifetime of a variable is the period during which it exists in memory. Local variables typically have a lifetime limited to the execution of the block or function in which they are declared, while global variables exist for the entire duration of the program.

2.1.5 Literals
In C, a **literal** is a fixed value that is explicitly specified in the code. Literals represent constant values that are used directly in the program without requiring any computation or storage in variables. They can be of various types, and here's an overview of the main categories of literals in C:
Types of Literals
1. **Integer Literals**
     - Represent whole numbers.
     - Can be in decimal, octal, or hexadecimal format.

Examples:
```
int a = 42;      // Decimal
int b = 052;     // Octal (equivalent to 42 in decimal)
int c = 0x2A;    // Hexadecimal (equivalent to 42 in decimal)
```
Floating-Point Literals
- Represent decimal numbers (floating-point).
- Can be written in standard or exponential notation.

Examples:
```
float x = 3.14;     // Standard notation
double y = 2.5e3;   // Exponential notation (2.5 × 10³ = 2500.0)
```
Character Literals
- Represent single characters enclosed in single quotes.
- They can also include escape sequences.

Examples:
```
char letter = 'A';      // Character literal
char newline = '\n';    // Escape sequence for newline
```
String Literals
- Represent sequences of characters enclosed in double quotes.
- String literals are automatically terminated with a null character ('\0').

Example:
```
char name[] = "Alice";  // String literal
```
2. **Boolean Literals** (in C99 and later)
    - Represent boolean values; true and false are defined in <stdbool.h>.

Example:
```
#include <stdbool.h>
bool isAvailable = true; // Boolean literal
```

Literals in C are constant values that you can use directly in your code. They come in various types, including integers, floating-point numbers, characters, and strings, each serving a specific purpose in programming. Understanding literals is essential for writing clear and effective C programs.

2.1.6 Comments

A comment is a portion of the code that is not executed by the compiler. Comments are used to leave notes, explanations, or annotations for anyone reading the code, including the original programmer. They can describe the purpose of the code, provide details about the logic, or leave reminders. Comments are hints that we add to our code, making it easier to understand. Comments are completely ignored by C compilers.

Types of Comments

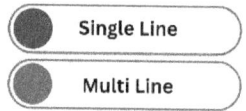

Single-line Comments in C

In C, a single line comment starts with // symbol. It starts and ends in the same line. For example,

```
#include <stdio.h>
int main() {
// create integer variable
  int age = 25;
// print the age variable
  printf("Age: %d", age);

  return 0;
}
```
Output
Age: 25

In the above example, we have used two single-line comments:

// create integer variable
// print the age variable

We can also use the single line comment along with the code.

int age = 25; // create integer variable

Here, code before // are executed and code after // are ignored by the compiler.

Multi-line Comments in C

In C programming, there is another type of comment that allows us to comment on multiple lines at once, they are multi-line comments.

To write multi-line comments, we use the /*....*/ symbol. For example,

```
/* This program takes age input from the user
It stores it in the age variable
And, print the value using printf() */

#include <stdio.h>
int main() {
// create integer variable
  int age = 25;
// print the age variable
  printf("Age: %d", age);
```

return 0;
}
Output
Age: 25

In this type of comment, the C compiler ignores everything from /* to */.

Why use Comments?
We should use comments for the following reasons:
Comments make our code readable for future reference.
Comments are used for debugging purposes.
We can use comments for code collaboration as it helps peer developers to understand our code.

Best Practices for Using Comments
- **Be Clear and Concise:** Write comments that are easy to understand and to the point.
- **Keep Comments Up-to-Date:** Ensure comments are updated when the code is modified.
- **Avoid Obvious Comments:** Don't state the obvious. For example, avoid comments like // increment i for i++;.
- **Use Descriptive Comments:** Explain the "why" and "how" rather than just the "what".

2.2 Input and Output Functions

In C programming, input and output (I/O) functions are essential for interacting with users and handling data. The standard library <stdio.h> provides several functions for this purpose, most notably printf() for output and scanf() for input.

2.2.1 scanf()

The scanf() function is used to read formatted input from the console. It requires the format specifiers to specify the type of data being read.

Syntax:
    scanf("%X", &variableOfXType);

where %X is the format specifier in C. It is a way to tell the compiler what type of data is in a variable and & is the address operator in C, which tells the compiler to change the real value of variableOfXType, stored at this address in the memory.

Example of scanf():
#include <stdio.h>
int main() {
    int age;
    float height;
    char name[50];

```c
    printf("Enter your name: ");
    scanf("%s", name);  // Read a string (no spaces)

    printf("Enter your age: ");
    scanf("%d", &age);  // Read an integer

    printf("Enter your height (in feet): ");
    scanf("%f", &height); // Read a float

    printf("\nName: %s\n", name);
    printf("Age: %d\n", age);
    printf("Height: %.1f feet\n", height);

    return 0;
}
```
Sample Input:
Enter your name: John
Enter your age: 30
Enter your height (in feet): 6.1
Output:
Name: John
Age: 30
Height: 6.1 feet

2.2.2 printf()
The printf() function is used to display formatted output on the console. It allows for various format specifiers to display different data types.
Syntax:
      printf("%X", variableOfXType);
where %X is the format specifier in C. It is a way to tell the compiler what type of data is in a variable and variableOfXType is the variable to be printed.
How to take input and output of basic types in C?
The basic type in C includes types like int, float, char, etc. Inorder to input or output the specific type, the X in the above syntax is changed with the specific format specifier of that type. The Syntax for input and output for these are:
Integer:
    Input: scanf("%d", &intVariable);
    Output: printf("%d", intVariable);
Float:
    Input: scanf("%f", &floatVariable);
    Output: printf("%f", floatVariable);
Character:
    Input: scanf("%c", &charVariable);

Output: printf("%c", charVariable);
Example of printf():
#include <stdio.h>

int main() {
   int age = 25;
   float height = 5.9;
   char name[] = "Alice";

   printf("Name: %s\n", name);
   printf("Age: %d\n", age);
   printf("Height: %.1f feet\n", height);

   return 0;
}
Output:
Name: Alice
Age: 25
Height: 5.9 feet

2.2.3 Format specifiers

A format specifier in C programming is a string that defines how data should be formatted for output or input operations. It tells functions like printf() and scanf() how to interpret the data types being handled. Format specifiers can control aspects like the type of data, its representation (e.g., decimal, hexadecimal), width, and precision. They provide a way to format the output and input of different data types.

Why format Specifiers

Format specifiers in C are used in input and output functions (like printf and scanf) to define the type and format of data being processed. They play a crucial role for several reasons:

1. Data Type Identification

Format specifiers help the functions understand what type of data to expect. For instance, %d is used for integers, %f for floating-point numbers, and %s for strings. This allows the compiler to interpret the data correctly.

2. Output Formatting

They allow you to control how the data is displayed. You can specify width, precision, padding, and alignment. For example:
- %5d ensures that the integer is right-aligned in a field of 5 characters.
- %.2f displays a floating-point number with two digits after the decimal point.

3. Input Handling

In functions like scanf, format specifiers tell the function what type of variable to store the input in, ensuring that the data is read correctly. For example, using %d expects an integer input and stores it in an int variable.

4. Type Safety
Using format specifiers provides a level of type safety by ensuring that the data types of the variables match the expected types, reducing the risk of runtime errors or unexpected behavior.

List of format specifiers with description and examples are given below:

Format Specifiers for Output (printf())

Specifier	Description	Example
%d	Signed integer (decimal)	printf("%d", 42);
%u	Unsigned integer	printf("%u", 42);
%f	Floating-point number	printf("%f", 3.14);
%e	Scientific notation (lowercase)	printf("%e", 3.14);
%E	Scientific notation (uppercase)	printf("%E", 3.14);
%g	Use %e or %f (whichever is shorter)	printf("%g", 3.14);
%G	Use %E or %f (whichever is shorter)	printf("%G", 3.14);
%c	Single character	printf("%c", 'A');
%s	String	printf("%s", "Hello");
%p	Pointer address	printf("%p", &var);
%x	Unsigned hexadecimal (lowercase)	printf("%x", 255);
%X	Unsigned hexadecimal (uppercase)	printf("%X", 255);
%o	Unsigned octal	printf("%o", 255);
%%	Print a literal %	printf("100%%");

Width and Precision Modifiers

You can also control the output's width and precision:
- **Width**: Specifies the minimum number of characters to output. If the output is shorter, it will be padded with spaces (or zeros, if specified).
- **Precision**: For floating-point numbers, this specifies the number of digits to display after the decimal point.

Example:
```
#include <stdio.h>
int main() {
   float pi = 3.14159;
  printf("Pi to 2 decimal places: %.2f\n", pi); // 3.14
  printf("Pi in a field of width 10: %10.2f\n", pi); // "     3.14"
  printf("Pi with minimum width 10, right-aligned: %10f\n", pi); // "  3.141590"

   return 0;
}
```
Format Specifiers for Input (scanf())

Specifier	Description	Example
%d	Reads a signed integer	scanf("%d", &var);
%u	Reads an unsigned integer	scanf("%u", &var);
%f	Reads a floating-point number	scanf("%f", &var);
%lf	Reads a double (floating-point)	scanf("%lf", &var);
%c	Reads a single character	scanf("%c", &var);
%s	Reads a string (until whitespace)	scanf("%s", str);
%x	Reads an unsigned hexadecimal integer	scanf("%x", &var);
%o	Reads an unsigned octal integer	scanf("%o", &var);

Example of Using Format Specifiers

Here's a complete example demonstrating both input and output format specifiers:

```
#include <stdio.h>
int main() {
    int age;
    float height;
    char name[50];

    // Input
    printf("Enter your name: ");
    scanf("%s", name);

    printf("Enter your age: ");
    scanf("%d", &age);

    printf("Enter your height (in feet): ");
    scanf("%f", &height);

    // Output
    printf("\nName: %s\n", name);
    printf("Age: %d years\n", age);
    printf("Height: %.1f feet\n", height);

    return 0;
}
```

Format specifiers in C are crucial for managing how data is presented and interpreted during input and output operations. Understanding these specifiers allows you to format your programs' I/O in a clear and effective manner, ensuring that data is displayed as intended and that user inputs are correctly captured.

CHAPTER 3: OPERATORS

3.1 Operators

3.1.1 Operators
In C programming, an **operator** is a special symbol that tells the compiler to perform specific mathematical, logical, or relational operations on operands (variables or values). Operators are fundamental components in programming that allow developers to manipulate data and perform calculations.
Examples: +, >>, *

3.1.2 Operands
An **operand** is a value or variable that an operator operates on. Operands can be of various types, including constants, variables, or expressions. They represent the data that the operator will manipulate or evaluate.
Examples:
>Integer : a=5
>Floating-point : b=3.14
>Character : c='A'

3.1.3 Expressions
An **expression** in C programming is a combination of variables, constants, operators, and function calls that evaluates to a single value. Expressions can be as simple as a single constant or variable, or they can be complex, involving multiple operators and operands.

Expression Types
In C programming, expressions can be classified into several types based on their functionality and the operations they perform.

- *Arithmetic Expressions*

These involve arithmetic operators and evaluate to a numeric value.
>**Operators**: +, -, *, /, %
>**Example**:
>int a = 5;
>int b = 10;
>int sum = a + b; // sum = 15

- *Relational Expressions*

These compare two values and evaluate to a boolean result (true or false).
>**Operators**: ==, !=, >, <, >=, <=
>**Example**:
>int a = 5;
>int b = 10;
>int isGreater = (a > b); // isGreater = 0 (false)

- *Logical Expressions*

These combine multiple relational expressions and evaluate to a boolean result.
 Operators: && (AND), || (OR), ! (NOT)
 Example:
 int a = 5;
 int b = 10;
 int c = 15;
 int result = (a < b) && (b < c); // result = 1 (true)
- *Bitwise Expressions*

These perform bit-level operations on integer types.
 Operators: & (AND), | (OR), ^ (XOR), ~ (NOT), << (left shift), >> (right shift)
 Example:
 int a = 5; // (binary: 0101)
 int b = 3; // (binary: 0011)
 int bitwiseResult = a & b; // bitwiseResult = 1 (binary: 0001)
- *Assignment Expressions*

These assign a value to a variable and evaluate to that value.
 Operator: =
 Example:
 int a;
 int assignmentResult = (a = 5); // a = 5, assignmentResult = 5

Conditional Expressions (Ternary Operator)

A shorthand for an if-else statement, which evaluates a condition and returns one of two values.
 Syntax: condition ? expression1 : expression2
 Example:
 int a = 5;
 int b = 10;
 int max = (a > b) ? a : b; // max = 10
- *Comma Expressions*

These evaluate multiple expressions where only one expression is expected. They evaluate from left to right, and the result is the value of the last expression.
 Example:
int a = (1, 2, 3); // a = 3
- *Function Call Expressions*

These call a function and evaluate to the value returned by the function.
 Example:
 int square(int x) {
 return x * x;
 }

 int result = square(5); // result = 25

Expressions in C can be simple or complex and can involve various types of operations. Understanding these different types of expressions is crucial for effective programming, as they form the basis of computations and logical reasoning in your code.

3.2 Types of Operators in C
They can be categorized into several types based on their functionality

3.2.1 Arithmetic Operators

Operator	Description	Example	Result
+	Addition	int sum = a + b;	Sum of a and b
-	Subtraction	int diff = a - b;	Difference of a and b
*	Multiplication	int product = a * b;	Product of a and b
/	Division	int quotient = a / b;	Quotient of a divided by b (integer division)
%	Modulus	int remainder = a % b;	Remainder of a divided by b

Example Program to demonstrating each arithmetic operator:

```c
#include <stdio.h>

int main() {
    int a = 10;
    int b = 3;

    // Addition
    int sum = a + b;         // 10 + 3 = 13
    printf("Sum: %d\n", sum);

    // Subtraction
    int diff = a - b;        // 10 - 3 = 7
    printf("Difference: %d\n", diff);

    // Multiplication
    int product = a * b;     // 10 * 3 = 30
    printf("Product: %d\n", product);

    // Division
    int quotient = a / b;    // 10 / 3 = 3 (integer division)
    printf("Quotient: %d\n", quotient);

    // Modulus
    int remainder = a % b;   // 10 % 3 = 1
    printf("Remainder: %d\n", remainder);
```

    return 0;
}
Output:
Sum: 13
Difference: 7
Product: 30
Quotient: 3
Remainder: 1
Notes
- **Integer Division**: When dividing two integers, the result is also an integer. Any fractional part is discarded. For example, 10 / 3 evaluates to 3, not 3.33.
- **Modulus Operator**: This operator only works with integer types and returns the remainder of a division. For instance, 10 % 3 gives 1 because 3 fits into 10 three times with a remainder of 1.

3.2.2 Increment and Decrement Operators

Operator	Description	Example	Result (if a = 5)
++	Increment Operator	++a (prefix)	6 (value is incremented before use)
		a++ (postfix)	5 (value is incremented after use)
--	Decrement Operator	--a (prefix)	4 (value is decremented before use)
		a-- (postfix)	5 (value is decremented after use)

Example program to demonstrating both increment and decrement operators:

```
#include <stdio.h>
int main() {
    int a = 5;

    // Prefix Increment
    int prefixIncrement = ++a;  // a is incremented to 6, then assigned to prefixIncrement
    printf("Prefix Increment: %d\n", prefixIncrement);  // Output: 6
    printf("Value of a after prefix increment: %d\n", a);  // Output: 6

    // Reset a for next example
    a = 5;

    // Postfix Increment
```

    int postfixIncrement = a++; // assigned to postfixIncrement, then a is incremented to 6
    printf("Postfix Increment: %d\n", postfixIncrement); // Output: 5
    printf("Value of a after postfix increment: %d\n", a); // Output: 6

    // Reset a for next example
    a = 5;

    // Prefix Decrement
    int prefixDecrement = --a; // a is decremented to 4, then assigned to prefixDecrement
    printf("Prefix Decrement: %d\n", prefixDecrement); // Output: 4
    printf("Value of a after prefix decrement: %d\n", a); // Output: 4

    // Reset a for next example
    a = 5;

    // Postfix Decrement
    int postfixDecrement = a--; // assigned to postfixDecrement, then a is decremented to 4
    printf("Postfix Decrement: %d\n", postfixDecrement); // Output: 5
    printf("Value of a after postfix decrement: %d\n", a); // Output: 4

    return 0;
}
```

Output
Prefix Increment: 6
Value of a after prefix increment: 6
Postfix Increment: 5
Value of a after postfix increment: 6
Prefix Decrement: 4
Value of a after prefix decrement: 4
Postfix Decrement: 5
Value of a after postfix decrement: 4

**Notes**
- **Prefix (++a / --a)**: The value of the variable is incremented or decremented before it is used in the expression.
- **Postfix (a++ / a--)**: The original value of the variable is used in the expression first, and then it is incremented or decremented.
- Both operators can be used with any numeric data type, including int, float, double, etc., but they are commonly used with integers.

Increment and decrement operators are essential for simplifying code that involves increasing or decreasing values by one. Understanding the difference
```

between prefix and postfix forms is crucial for predicting the behavior of expressions in your programs.

3.2.3 Relational Operators

Relational operators in C are used to compare two values or expressions. They return a boolean value (true or false), which is useful in control flow statements such as if conditions or loops.

Operator	Description	Example	Result (if a = 5, b = 10)
==	Equal to	a == b	false (0)
!=	Not equal to	a != b	true (1)
>	Greater than	a > b	false (0)
<	Less than	a < b	true (1)
>=	Greater than or equal to	a >= b	false (0)
<=	Less than or equal to	a <= b	true (1)

Example Program demonstrating each relational operators:

```
#include <stdio.h>

int main() {
    int a = 5;
    int b = 10;

    // Equal to
    printf("a == b: %d\n", (a == b));  // Output: 0 (false)

    // Not equal to
    printf("a != b: %d\n", (a != b));  // Output: 1 (true)

    // Greater than
    printf("a > b: %d\n", (a > b));   // Output: 0 (false)

    // Less than
    printf("a < b: %d\n", (a < b));   // Output: 1 (true)

    // Greater than or equal to
    printf("a >= b: %d\n", (a >= b));  // Output: 0 (false)

    // Less than or equal to
    printf("a <= b: %d\n", (a <= b));  // Output: 1 (true)

    return 0;
}
```
Output
a == b: 0

a != b: 1
a > b: 0
a < b: 1
a >= b: 0
a <= b: 1

Notes
- **Boolean Values**: In C, true is represented by 1 and false is represented by 0.
- **Data Types**: Relational operators can be used with various data types, including integers, floating-point numbers, and characters.
- **Short-Circuit Evaluation**: In compound logical expressions, evaluation stops as soon as the result is determined (e.g., if one operand of an && operation is false).

Relational operators are essential for making comparisons in C. They are commonly used in control flow statements to execute code conditionally based on comparisons between values. Understanding how to use these operators effectively is crucial for writing logic in C programs.

3.2.4 Assignment Operators

Assignment operators in C are used to assign values to variables. The most basic assignment operator is =, but there are also several compound assignment operators that combine assignment with arithmetic operations. Here's a detailed explanation in tabular format:

Operator	Description	Example	Equivalent to
=	Simple assignment	a = 5;	a is assigned the value 5
+=	Add and assign	a += 3;	a = a + 3;
-=	Subtract and assign	a -= 2;	a = a - 2;
*=	Multiply and assign	a *= 4;	a = a * 4;
/=	Divide and assign	a /= 2;	a = a / 2;
%=	Modulus and assign	a %= 3;	a = a % 3;
<<=	Left shift and assign	a <<= 1;	a = a << 1;
>>=	Right shift and assign	a >>= 1;	a = a >> 1;
&=	Bitwise AND and assign	a &= 3;	a = a & 3;
`=`	`=`	Bitwise OR and assign	`a
^=	Bitwise XOR and assign	a ^= 3;	a = a ^ 3;

Example demonstrating various assignment operators:
#include <stdio.h>

```c
int main() {
    int a = 10;

    // Simple assignment
    printf("Initial value of a: %d\n", a);  // Output: 10

    // Add and assign
    a += 5;  // a = 10 + 5
    printf("After += 5: %d\n", a);  // Output: 15

    // Subtract and assign
    a -= 3;  // a = 15 - 3
    printf("After -= 3: %d\n", a);  // Output: 12

    // Multiply and assign
    a *= 2;  // a = 12 * 2
    printf("After *= 2: %d\n", a);  // Output: 24

    // Divide and assign
    a /= 4;  // a = 24 / 4
    printf("After /= 4: %d\n", a);  // Output: 6

    // Modulus and assign
    a %= 5;  // a = 6 % 5
    printf("After %= 5: %d\n", a);  // Output: 1

    // Left shift and assign
    a <<= 1;  // a = 1 << 1
    printf("After <<= 1: %d\n", a);  // Output: 2

    // Right shift and assign
    a >>= 1;  // a = 2 >> 1
    printf("After >>= 1: %d\n", a);  // Output: 1

    return 0;
}
```
Output
Initial value of a: 10
After += 5: 15
After -= 3: 12
After *= 2: 24
After /= 4: 6

After %= 5: 1
After <<= 1: 2
After >>= 1: 1

Notes
- **Compound Assignment**: The compound assignment operators (like +=, -=, etc.) are shorthand for updating a variable's value without repeating the variable name.
- **Types**: Assignment operators can be used with various data types, including integers, floats, and doubles.
- **Left and Right Shift**: The shift operators (<< and >>) are used to shift bits left or right, effectively multiplying or dividing by powers of two.

Assignment operators are fundamental in C for assigning and modifying the values of variables. Understanding these operators is essential for writing efficient and concise code.

3.2.5 Logical Operators

These operators returns Boolean value either **True** or **False**. Logical operators are used to combine multiple conditional statements (relational) to evaluate the **truth** value of the resulting expression. Logical operators "not", "and", "or" truth tables as given below:

not Truth Table	
Relation (A)	not A
True	False
False	True

"or" Truth Table for 2 Relations		
Relation (A)	Relation (B)	A or B
True	True	True
True	False	True
False	True	True
False	False	False

"and" Truth Table for 2 Relations		
Relation (A)	Relation (B)	A and B
True	True	True
True	False	False
False	True	False
False	False	False

Operator	Description	Example	Result (if a = 1, b = 0)
&&	Logical AND	a && b	0 (false)
||	Logical OR	a || b	1(True)
!	Logical NOT	!a	0 (false)

Following table with example values for logical operators with relational operators :

S. No	Symbol	Name	Example a=10, b=3 x=20, y=50	Out put	Explanation
1	||	Logical or	a<b || x<y	True	False or True=>True
2	&&	Logical and	a>b && x<y	True	True and True=>True
3	!	Logical not	!(a<b or x<y)	False	Not (True)=>False

Example demonstrating each logical operator in a C program:
#include <stdio.h>

int main() {
   int a = 1; // true (non-zero)
   int b = 0; // false (zero)

   // Logical AND
   if (a && b) {
      printf("Both a and b are true.\n");
   } else {
      printf("At least one of a or b is false.\n"); // This will execute
   }

   // Logical OR
   if (a || b) {
      printf("At least one of a or b is true.\n"); // This will execute
   } else {
      printf("Both a and b are false.\n");
   }

   // Logical NOT
   if (!a) {
      printf("a is false.\n");
   } else {

        printf("a is true.\n"); // This will execute
    }

    return 0;
}
Output
At least one of a or b is false.
At least one of a or b is true.
a is true.
Notes
- **Logical AND (&&)**: Returns true (1) if both operands are true. If either operand is false, it returns false (0).
- **Logical OR (||)**: Returns true (1) if at least one of the operands is true. It returns false (0) only if both operands are false.
- **Logical NOT (!)**: Inverts the boolean value of the operand. If the operand is true, it returns false; if false, it returns true.
- **Short-Circuit Evaluation**: In logical expressions, evaluation stops as soon as the result is determined. For example, in a && b, if a is false, b will not be evaluated because the entire expression cannot be true.

Example demonstrating each logical operator with relational operators:
This program will use relational operators to compare two integers and then use logical operators to evaluate the conditions.

```
#include <stdio.h>
int main() {
    int a = 5;
    int b = 10;
    int c = 15;

    // Using relational operators with logical AND (&&)
    if (a < b && b < c) {
        printf("Both conditions are true: a is less than b and b is less than c.\n");
    } else {
        printf("At least one condition is false.\n");
    }

    // Using relational operators with logical OR (||)
    if (a > b || b < c) {
        printf("At least one condition is true: a is greater than b or b is less than c.\n");
    } else {
        printf("Both conditions are false.\n");
    }
```

```c
// Using relational operator with logical NOT (!)
if (!(a > b)) {
    printf("a is not greater than b.\n");  // This will execute
}

return 0;
}
```
Output
Both conditions are true: a is less than b and b is less than c.
At least one condition is true: a is greater than b or b is less than c.
a is not greater than b.

Explanation
1. **Logical AND (&&):**
   - The expression a < b && b < c checks if both conditions are true. Since 5 < 10 and 10 < 15, this condition is true, and the corresponding message is printed.
2. **Logical OR (||):**
   - The expression a > b || b < c checks if at least one of the conditions is true. Since 5 > 10 is false but 10 < 15 is true, the overall expression is true, and the corresponding message is printed.
3. **Logical NOT (!):**
   - The expression !(a > b) checks if a is not greater than b. Since 5 is not greater than 10, this condition is true, and the message is printed.

By combining logical operators with relational operators, you can create more complex and nuanced conditions in your C programs. This allows for more precise control over program flow and decision-making.

Logical operators are essential for controlling the flow of execution in C programs. They allow you to build complex conditional statements and perform decision-making based on multiple criteria. Understanding how these operators work is crucial for effective programming.

3.2.6 Bitwise Operators

Bitwise operators in C are used to perform operations on the individual bits of integer types. In the binary, it treated 1 as True and 0 as False. Python execution environment internally it converts integer into binary and performs the *"bit to bit"* operation on two integers and it gives us result as integer. Truth tables of bitwise &, |, ^(XOR) operators as given below:

Bitwise	Truth Table for 2 bits

Bit (A)	Bit (B)	A | B
1	1	1
1	0	1
0	1	1
0	0	0

Bitwise & Truth Table for 2 bits

Bit (A)	Bit (B)	A & B
1	1	1
1	0	0
0	1	0
0	0	0

Bitwise XOR Truth Table for 2 bits

Bit (A)	Bit (B)	A ^ B
1	1	0
1	0	1
0	1	1
0	0	0

Description of bitwise operators with example are given in table:

Operator	Description	Example	Result (if a = 5 (0101), b = 3 (0011))
&	Bitwise AND	a & b	1 (0001)
|	Bitwise OR	Bitwise OR	5 (0101)
^	Bitwise XOR	a ^ b	6 (0110)
~	Bitwise NOT	~a	-6 (1010 in 2's complement)
<<	Left Shift	a << 1	10 (1010)
>>	Right Shift	a >> 1	2 (0010)

Complete example demonstrating each bitwise operator:

```
#include <stdio.h>
int main() {
    int a = 5;  // Binary: 0101
    int b = 3;  // Binary: 0011

    // Bitwise AND
    int and_result = a & b; // 0101 & 0011 = 0001
```

```c
    printf("Bitwise AND (a & b): %d\n", and_result);  // Output: 1

    // Bitwise OR
    int or_result = a | b;   // 0101 | 0011 = 0111
    printf("Bitwise OR (a | b): %d\n", or_result);   // Output: 7

    // Bitwise XOR
    int xor_result = a ^ b;  // 0101 ^ 0011 = 0110
    printf("Bitwise XOR (a ^ b): %d\n", xor_result);  // Output: 6

    // Bitwise NOT
    int not_result = ~a;    // ~0101 = 1010 (in 2's complement, this is -6)
    printf("Bitwise NOT (~a): %d\n", not_result);    // Output: -6

    // Left Shift
    int left_shift_result = a << 1; // 0101 << 1 = 1010
    printf("Left Shift (a << 1): %d\n", left_shift_result); // Output: 10

    // Right Shift
    int right_shift_result = a >> 1; // 0101 >> 1 = 0010
    printf("Right Shift (a >> 1): %d\n", right_shift_result); // Output: 2

    return 0;
}
```

Output
Bitwise AND (a & b): 1
Bitwise OR (a | b): 7
Bitwise XOR (a ^ b): 6
Bitwise NOT (~a): -6
Left Shift (a << 1): 10
Right Shift (a >> 1): 2

Explanation of Bitwise Operators
1. **Bitwise AND (&):**
    - **Description**: Compares each bit of two operands; returns 1 if both bits are 1.
    - **Example**: 5 & 3 gives 1 because 0101 & 0011 = 0001.
2. **Bitwise OR (|):**
    - **Description**: Compares each bit of two operands; returns 1 if at least one bit is 1.
    - **Example**: 5 | 3 gives 7 because 0101 | 0011 = 0111.
3. **Bitwise XOR (^):**
    - **Description**: Compares each bit of two operands; returns 1 if the bits are different.

- **Example**: 5 ^ 3 gives 6 because 0101 ^ 0011 = 0110.
4. **Bitwise NOT (~)**:
   - **Description**: Inverts all bits of the operand.
   - **Example**: ~5 results in -6 because the binary representation of 5 is 0101, and ~0101 is 1010 (in 2's complement).
5. **Left Shift (<<)**:
   - **Description**: Shifts the bits of the left operand to the left by the number of positions specified by the right operand. Fills the new rightmost bits with 0.
   - **Example**: 5 << 1 gives 10 because 0101 << 1 is 1010.
6. **Right Shift (>>)**:
   - **Description**: Shifts the bits of the left operand to the right by the number of positions specified by the right operand. Fills the new leftmost bits with the sign bit (0 for positive numbers).
   - **Example**: 5 >> 1 gives 2 because 0101 >> 1 is 0010.

Bitwise operators are powerful tools for manipulating individual bits of data in C. They are commonly used in low-level programming, such as embedded systems and performance-critical applications. Understanding these operators is essential for efficient programming and optimization techniques.

3.2.7 Conditional (Ternary) Operator

The ternary operator in C is a shorthand for the if-else statement and is used for conditional expressions. It is also known as the conditional operator and is represented by the symbol ? :

Operator	Description	Example	Result (if x = 5)
? :	Conditional operator (ternary)	x > 10 ? "Greater" : "Less"	"Less"

Syntax:
    condition ? expression_if_true : expression_if_false;

Complete example demonstrating the ternary operator:
```
#include <stdio.h>

int main() {
    int x = 5;

    // Using the ternary operator
    const char* result = (x > 10) ? "Greater" : "Less or Equal";

    printf("The value of x is: %s\n", result); // Output: Less or Equal

    // Another example with a numeric condition
    int max = (x > 10) ? x : 10;
```

```c
printf("The maximum value is: %d\n", max);  // Output: 10

    return 0;
}
```
Output
The value of x is: Less or Equal
The maximum value is: 10

Explanation of the Ternary Operator
1. **Conditional Evaluation**: The condition (x > 10) is evaluated first.
   - If true, the expression before the colon ("Greater") is executed.
   - If false, the expression after the colon ("Less or Equal") is executed.
2. **Assignment**: The result of the ternary operation can be assigned to a variable. In this example, the result is stored in the variable result.
3. **Usage for Maximum Value**: The ternary operator can also be used for other expressions, such as determining the maximum of two values. Here, if x is greater than 10, max is assigned x; otherwise, it gets the value 10.

The ternary operator is a concise way to express conditional logic in C. It can help make the code cleaner and more readable for simple conditions. However, for more complex conditions or multiple statements, using traditional if-else constructs may be more appropriate for clarity.

3.2.8 Other Operators

(a) Comma Operator

Operator	Description	Example	Result
,	Evaluates two expressions and returns the value of the second	int a = (2, 3);	a = 3

Example
```c
#include <stdio.h>
int main() {
    int a, b;
    a = (1, 2); // evaluates to 2
    b = (3, 4, 5); // evaluates to 5
    printf("a = %d, b = %d\n", a, b); // Output: a = 2, b = 5
    return 0;
}
```
Output
a = 2, b = 5

(b) Sizeof Operator

Operator	Description	Example	Result
sizeof	Returns the size of a data type or variable in bytes	sizeof(int)	4 (on most systems)

Example

```c
#include <stdio.h>
int main() {
    int x;
    double y;
    printf("Size of int: %zu bytes\n", sizeof(x));   // Output: Size of int: 4 bytes
    printf("Size of double: %zu bytes\n", sizeof(y)); // Output: Size of double: 8 bytes
    return 0;
}
```

Output
Size of int: 4 bytes
Size of double: 8 bytes

(c) Pointer Operators

Operator	Description	Example	Result
*	Dereference operator (access value at pointer)	int *p; *p = 10;	value at p is 10
&	Address-of operator (get address of variable)	int x; &x	address of x

Example
```c
#include <stdio.h>
int main() {
    int x = 10;
    int *p = &x;  // p holds the address of x
    printf("Value of x: %d\n", *p);  // Output: Value of x: 10
    printf("Address of x: %p\n", (void*)&x); // Output: Address of x
    return 0;
}
```

Output
Value of x: 10
Address of x: <address>

(d) Member Access Operators

Operator	Description	Example	Result
.	Direct member access for structures/classes	struct s { int x; }; s1.x = 5;	Access x in s1
->	Indirect member access for pointers to structures	p->x	Access x from struct pointed to by p

Example
```c
#include <stdio.h>

struct Point {
    int x;
```

```c
    int y;
};

int main() {
    struct Point p1;
    struct Point *p2 = &p1;

    p1.x = 10;       // Using dot operator
    p2->y = 20;      // Using arrow operator

    printf("p1.x = %d, p2->y = %d\n", p1.x, p2->y); // Output: p1.x = 10, p2->y = 20
    return 0;
}
```
Output
p1.x = 10, p2->y = 20

(e) Type Cast Operator

Operator	Description	Example	Result
(type)	Converts a value from one type to another	(float)5	5.0 (float representation)

Example
```c
#include <stdio.h>

int main() {
    int a = 5;
    float b = (float)a / 2;  // Type cast to float
    printf("Result: %.2f\n", b); // Output: Result: 2.50
    return 0;
}
```
Output
Result: 2.50

Summary
- **Comma Operator**: Evaluates two expressions and returns the second.
- **Sizeof Operator**: Determines the size of a data type or variable in bytes.
- **Pointer Operators**: Used for dereferencing and obtaining the address of variables.
- **Member Access Operators**: Access members of structures or classes directly or via pointers.
- **Type Cast Operator**: Converts one data type to another, ensuring correct type handling in expressions.

These operators are fundamental in C programming, enabling various functionalities from memory management to type manipulation.

Example Programs

1. Write a C Program to read the radius of a circle, calculate its area and display it.

```c
#include <stdio.h>

int main() {
    float radius, area;
    const float PI = 3.14;

    printf("Enter the radius of the circle: ");
    scanf("%f", &radius);

    area = PI * radius * radius;
    printf("Area of the circle: %.2f\n", area);

    return 0;
}
```
Enter the radius of the circle: 5
Area of the circle: 78.50

2. Write a C Program read p, n, r and calculate Simple Interest.

```c
#include <stdio.h>

int main() {
    float p, n, r, simpleInterest;

    printf("Enter principal amount (P): ");
    scanf("%f", &p);
    printf("Enter time period in years (N): ");
    scanf("%f", &n);
    printf("Enter rate of interest (R): ");
    scanf("%f", &r);

    simpleInterest = (p * n * r) / 100;
    printf("Simple Interest: %.2f\n", simpleInterest);

    return 0;
}
```
Enter principal amount (P): 1000
Enter time period in years (N): 2
Enter rate of interest (R): 5
Simple Interest: 100.00

3. Write a C Program to calculate Compound Interest.

```c
#include <stdio.h>
#include <math.h>

int main() {
    float principal, rate, time, amount, compoundInterest;

    printf("Enter principal amount: ");
    scanf("%f", &principal);
    printf("Enter rate of interest: ");
    scanf("%f", &rate);
    printf("Enter time (in years): ");
    scanf("%f", &time);

    amount = principal * pow((1 + rate / 100), time);
    compoundInterest = amount - principal;
    printf("Compound Interest: %.2f\n", compoundInterest);

    return 0;
}
```
Enter principal amount: 1000
Enter rate of interest: 5
Enter time (in years): 2
Compound Interest: 102.50

4. **WACP to calculate the Sum of N natural numbers**

```c
#include <stdio.h>

int main() {
    int n;
    int sum;

    // Prompt the user for input
    printf("Enter a positive integer N: ");
    scanf("%d", &n);

    // Calculate the sum using the formula
    sum = (n * (n + 1)) / 2;

    // Display the result
    printf("Sum of the first %d natural numbers: %d\n", n, sum);

    return 0;
}
```
Enter a positive integer N: 5

Sum of the first 5 natural numbers: 15

5. WACP to calculate Sum of squares of n natural numbers

```c
#include <stdio.h>

int main() {
    int n;
    int sum_of_squares;

    // Prompt the user for input
    printf("Enter a positive integer N: ");
    scanf("%d", &n);

    // Calculate the sum of squares using the formula
    sum_of_squares = (n * (n + 1) * (2 * n + 1)) / 6;

    // Display the result
    printf("Sum of the squares of the first %d natural numbers: %d\n", n, sum_of_squares);

    return 0;
}
```
Enter a positive integer N: 3
Sum of the squares of the first 3 natural numbers: 14

6. WACP to convert Celsius to Fahrenheit, vice versa conversion

Celsius to Fahrenheit

```c
#include <stdio.h>

int main() {
    float celsius, fahrenheit;

    // Prompt the user for input
    printf("Enter temperature in Celsius: ");
    scanf("%f", &celsius);

    // Convert Celsius to Fahrenheit
    fahrenheit = (celsius * 9/5) + 32;

    // Display the result
    printf("Temperature in Fahrenheit: %.2f\n", fahrenheit);

    return 0;
}
```
Output

Enter temperature in Celsius: 100
Temperature in Fahrenheit: 212.00

Fahrenheit to Celsius

```c
#include <stdio.h>

int main() {
    float fahrenheit, celsius;

    // Prompt the user for input
    printf("Enter temperature in Fahrenheit: ");
    scanf("%f", &fahrenheit);

    // Convert Fahrenheit to Celsius
    celsius = (fahrenheit - 32) * 5/9;

    // Display the result
    printf("Temperature in Celsius: %.2f\n", celsius);

    return 0;
}
```

Output:
Enter temperature in Fahrenheit: 212
Temperature in Celsius: 100.00

7. WACP to Finding Big and small among two values using ternary operator

```c
#include <stdio.h>

int main() {
    int a, b;

    printf("Enter two values: ");
    scanf("%d %d", &a, &b);

    (a > b) ? printf("Big: %d, Small: %d\n", a, b) : printf("Big: %d, Small: %d\n", b, a);

    return 0;
}
```

Output:
Enter two values: 10 20
Big: 20, Small: 10

8. WACP to Finding Big and small among three values using ternary operator

```
#include <stdio.h>

int main() {
    int a, b, c;

    printf("Enter three values: ");
    scanf("%d %d %d", &a, &b, &c);

    int big = (a > b) ? (a > c ? a : c) : (b > c ? b : c);
    int small = (a < b) ? (a < c ? a : c) : (b < c ? b : c);

    printf("Big: %d, Small: %d\n", big, small);

    return 0;
}
```
Output:
Enter three values: 10 20 5
Big: 20, Small: 5

8. WACP to Finding Big and small among four values using ternary operator

```
#include <stdio.h>

int main() {
    int a, b, c, d;

    printf("Enter four values: ");
    scanf("%d %d %d %d", &a, &b, &c, &d);

    int big = (a > b) ? (a > c ? (a > d ? a : d) : (c > d ? c : d)) : (b > c ? (b > d ? b : d) : (c > d ? c : d));
    int small = (a < b) ? (a < c ? (a < d ? a : d) : (c < d ? c : d)) : (b < c ? (b < d ? b : d) : (c < d ? c : d));

    printf("Big: %d, Small: %d\n", big, small);

    return 0;
}
```
Output:
Enter four values: 10 20 5 15
Big: 20, Small: 5

9. **Write a C program to check whether a number is even or odd using ternary operator**

```
#include <stdio.h>

int main() {
    int num;

    printf("Enter a number: ");
    scanf("%d", &num);

    (num % 2 == 0) ? printf("%d is even\n", num) : printf("%d is odd\n", num);

    return 0;
}
```
Output:
Enter a number: 7
7 is odd

10. **Write a C program to check and print whether a user is eligible to vote using ternary operator**

```
#include <stdio.h>

int main() {
    int age;

    printf("Enter your age: ");
    scanf("%d", &age);

    (age >= 18) ? printf("Eligible to vote\n") : printf("Not eligible to vote\n");

    return 0;
}
```
Output:
Enter your age: 16
Not eligible to vote

11. **WACP to Swap two values using 3rd variable using ternary operator.**

```
#include <stdio.h>

int main() {
    int a, b, temp;

    printf("Enter two values: ");
    scanf("%d %d", &a, &b);
```

```
    temp = a;
    a = b;
    b = temp;

    printf("After swapping: a = %d, b = %d\n", a, b);

    return 0;
}
```
Output:
Enter two values: 5 10
After swapping: a = 10, b = 5

12. WACP to Swap two values without using 3rd variable

```
#include <stdio.h>

int main() {
    int a, b;

    printf("Enter two values: ");
    scanf("%d %d", &a, &b);

    a = a + b;
    b = a - b;
    a = a - b;

    printf("After swapping: a = %d, b = %d\n", a, b);

    return 0;
}
```
Output:
Enter two values: 5 10
After swapping: a = 10, b = 5

13. Write a C Program to check whether a given year is a leap year or not using ternary operator

```
#include <stdio.h>

int main() {
    int year;

    // Prompt the user for input
    printf("Enter a year: ");
    scanf("%d", &year);
```

```c
    // Check if the year is a leap year using ternary operator
    (year % 4 == 0 && (year % 100 != 0 || year % 400 == 0))
        ? printf("%d is a leap year.\n", year)
        : printf("%d is not a leap year.\n", year);

    return 0;
}
```
Output:
Enter a year: 2020
2020 is a leap year.
Enter a year: 1900
1900 is not a leap year.

CHAPTER 4: CONTROL STATEMENTS

4.1 Control Statements

Control statements in C are constructs that dictate the flow of execution of the program based on certain conditions or repeatedly execute blocks of code. They allow you to implement decision-making and looping behavior, enabling the program to respond differently based on various inputs or conditions.

4.1.1 Types of Control Statements

In C, control statements can be categorized into three main types based on their functionality:

(a) Conditional Statements
 if, if-else, nested if-if, if else ladder, switch,nested switch
(b) Looping Statements
 for loop, while loop, do-while
(c) Jump Statements
 break,continue, goto,return

4.2 Conditional Statements

These are also called decision-making statements. A conditional statement is used to make decisions based on certain conditions. It allows the program to execute a certain block of code if a condition is true, and a different block of code if the condition is false. Conditional statements perform a certain operation one time when a condition is true or false
Let us X and Y are two operations
 # Perform X-Operation in the case of True (or)
 # Perform Y-Operation in the case of False

Example 1:
 Do you have money more than 50,000?: Yes/True
  Then Buy Laptop
 Do you have money more than 50,000? No/False?
  Then, Buy Desktop

Examples 2:
 Is number divisible by 2 ?: Yes/True
 Then, Number is Even
 Is number divisible by 2? No/False
  Then, Number is Odd

Example 3:
 Is student percentage greater than or equal to 35? True
  Then, Student Passed in the exam

Is student percentage greater than or equal to 35? False
Then, Student Failed in the exam

4.2.1 if statement
An **if** statement consists of a boolean expression followed by one or more statements.
The if statement is used for deciding between two paths based on a True or False outcome. It is represented by the following flowchart –

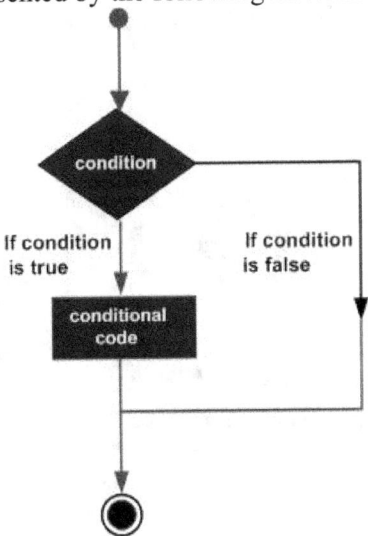

Syntax
if (Boolean expr){
   expression;
   . . .
}
An **if** statement consists of a boolean expression followed by one or more statements.

Example: Check if a number is positive
```
#include <stdio.h>
int main() {
   int number;

   printf("Enter a number: ");
   scanf("%d", &number);

   if (number > 0) {
      printf("The number is positive.\n");
   }
```

return 0;
}
Output
Enter a number: 5
The number is positive.

4.2.2 If-else Statement

An **if** statement can be followed by an optional **else** statement, which executes when the Boolean expression is false.

The if–else statement offers an alternative path when the condition isn't met.

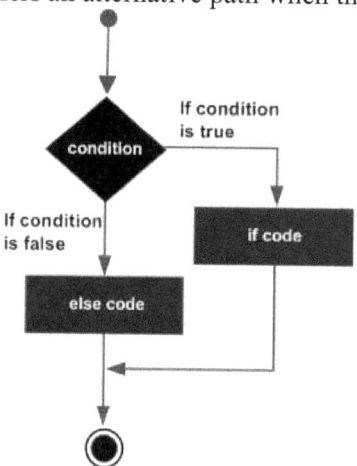

An **if** statement can be followed by an optional **else** statement, which executes when the Boolean expression is false.

Syntax
if (Boolean expr){
   expression;
   . . .
}
else{
   expression;
   . . .
}

Example: Check if a number is even or odd
#include <stdio.h>

int main() {
   int number;

   printf("Enter a number: ");
   scanf("%d", &number);

```
if (number % 2 == 0) {
   printf("The number is even.\n");
} else {
   printf("The number is odd.\n");
}

return 0;
}
```
Output
Enter a number: 7
The number is odd.

4.2.3 if-else if or if else ladder

The if-else-if ladder statement is an extension to the if-else statement. It is used in the scenario where there are multiple cases to be performed for different conditions. In if-else-if ladder statement, if a condition is true then the statements defined in the if block will be executed, otherwise if some other condition is true then the statements defined in the else-if block will be executed, at the last if none of the condition is true then the statements defined in the else block will be executed. There are multiple else-if blocks possible. It is similar to the switch case statement where the default is executed instead of else block if none of the cases is matched

Flow chart of if else ladder is

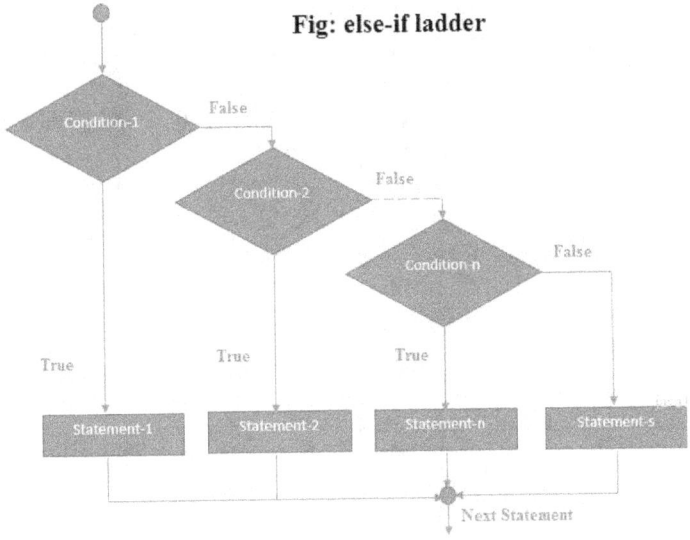

Fig: else-if ladder

An example of if else ladder flow chart to determine the student grade based on percentage is given below:

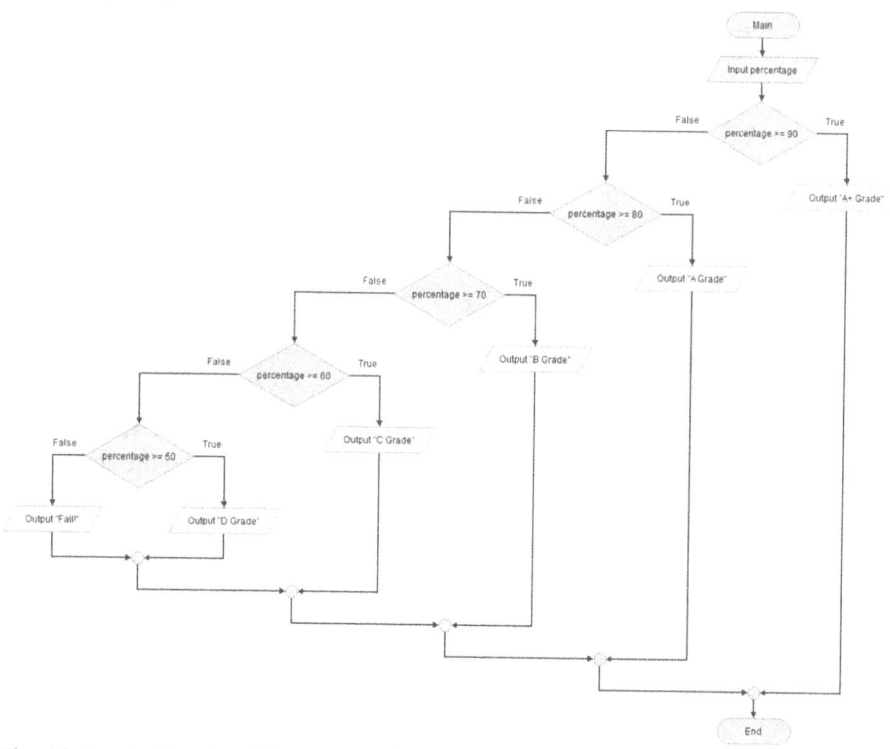

The if-else ladder in C is a control structure that allows you to check multiple conditions sequentially. It is used when you have several conditions to evaluate and each condition requires a different block of code to execute based on the result. The ladder consists of multiple if statements followed by one or more else if statements, with an optional else at the end.

Syntax
if(condition1){
//code to be executed if condition1 is true
}else if(condition2){
//code to be executed if condition2 is true
}
else if(condition3){
//code to be executed if condition3 is true
}
...
else{
//code to be executed if all the conditions are false
}

Example: Grade Classification
Here's an example of an if-else ladder that classifies student grades based on their marks:

c
Copy code
```
#include <stdio.h>

int main() {
    int marks;

    printf("Enter your marks: ");
    scanf("%d", &marks);

    if (marks >= 90) {
        printf("Grade: A\n");
    } else if (marks >= 80) {
        printf("Grade: B\n");
    } else if (marks >= 70) {
        printf("Grade: C\n");
    } else if (marks >= 60) {
        printf("Grade: D\n");
    } else {
        printf("Grade: F\n");
    }

    return 0;
}
```

Output
Enter your marks: 85
Grade: B

How It Works
1. **Condition Evaluation**: The program checks each condition in order:
    - If marks >= 90, it prints "Grade: A".
    - If the first condition is false, it checks marks >= 80, and so on.
2. **Execution**: Once a true condition is found, the corresponding block of code is executed, and the remaining conditions are not checked.
3. **Final else**: If none of the conditions are true, the else block executes, which in this case gives a grade of F for marks below 60.

4.2.4 nested if else
You can use one **if** or **else-if** statement inside another **if** or **else-if** statement(s). Nested if statements are required to build intricate decision trees, evaluating multiple nested conditions for nuanced program flow.

Flow chart

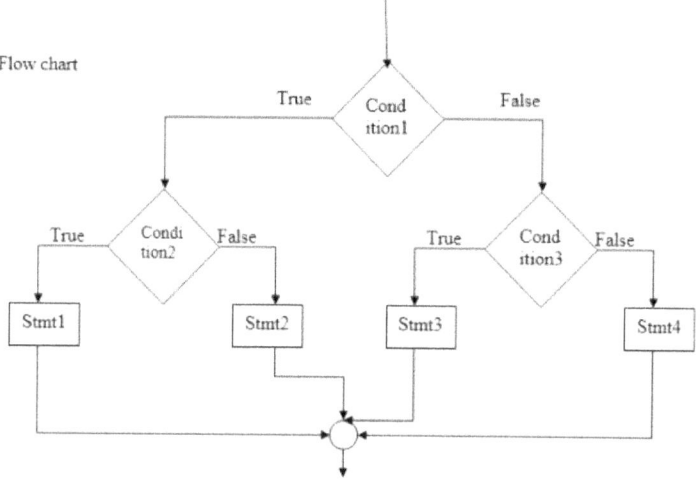

You can use one **if** or **else-if** statement inside another **if** or **else-if** statement(s). A **nested if-else** statement is used when you need to evaluate a condition inside another if or else block. This allows for more complex decision-making.

Syntax
```
if (condition1) {
    // Code to execute if condition1 is true
    if (condition2) {
        // Code to execute if condition2 is true
    } else {
        // Code to execute if condition2 is false
    }
} else {
    // Code to execute if condition1 is false
}
```

Example 1: Check Age and Voting Eligibility
```
#include <stdio.h>

int main() {
    int age;

    printf("Enter your age: ");
    scanf("%d", &age);

    if (age >= 18) {
        printf("You are eligible to vote.\n");
        if (age < 65) {
            printf("You are eligible for regular voting.\n");
        } else {
```

```c
      printf("You are eligible for senior voting.\n");
    }
  } else {
    printf("You are not eligible to vote.\n");
  }

  return 0;
}
```
Output
Enter your age: 70
You are eligible to vote.
You are eligible for senior voting.

Example 2: Grade Classification with Nested Conditions
```c
#include <stdio.h>
int main() {
  int marks;

  printf("Enter your marks: ");
  scanf("%d", &marks);

  if (marks >= 0 && marks <= 100) { // Check for valid range
    if (marks >= 90) {
      printf("Grade: A\n");
    } else if (marks >= 80) {
      printf("Grade: B\n");
    } else if (marks >= 70) {
      printf("Grade: C\n");
    } else if (marks >= 60) {
      printf("Grade: D\n");
    } else {
      printf("Grade: F\n");
    }
  } else {
    printf("Invalid marks. Please enter a value between 0 and 100.\n");
  }

  return 0;
}
```
Output
Enter your marks: 85
Grade: B

4.2.5 Switch Statement
A switch statement simplifies multi-way choices by evaluating a single variable against multiple values, executing specific code based on the match. It allows a variable to be tested for equality against a list of values.

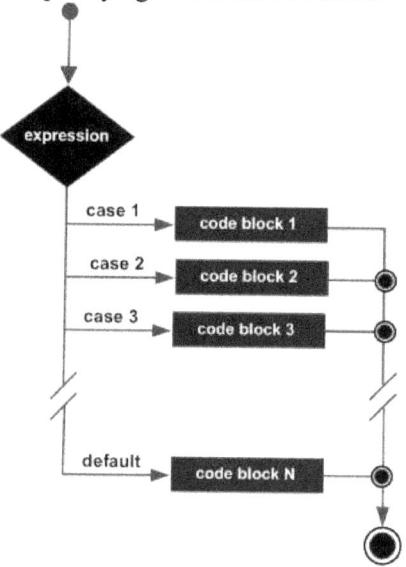

Syntax
```
switch (expression) {
  case constant1:
    // Code to execute if expression == constant1
    break;
  case constant2:
    // Code to execute if expression == constant2
    break;
  // Add more cases as needed
  default:
    // Code to execute if none of the cases match
}
```
Key Points
- **Expression**: The expression evaluated in the switch statement should return an integer value or an enumeration constant.
- **Case**: Each case represents a constant value. If the expression matches this value, the corresponding block of code executes.
- **Break**: The break statement is used to exit the switch block. If omitted, execution will "fall through" to the next case.
- **Default**: The default case is optional and executes if none of the specified cases match the expression.

Example 1: Day of the Week
```c
#include <stdio.h>

int main() {
    int day;

    printf("Enter a number (1-7) for the day of the week: ");
    scanf("%d", &day);

    switch (day) {
        case 1:
            printf("Monday\n");
            break;
        case 2:
            printf("Tuesday\n");
            break;
        case 3:
            printf("Wednesday\n");
            break;
        case 4:
            printf("Thursday\n");
            break;
        case 5:
            printf("Friday\n");
            break;
        case 6:
            printf("Saturday\n");
            break;
        case 7:
            printf("Sunday\n");
            break;
        default:
            printf("Invalid input! Please enter a number between 1 and 7.\n");
    }

    return 0;
}
```
Output
Enter a number (1-7) for the day of the week: 3
Wednesday

Example: Calculator Using Switch
```c
#include <stdio.h>
```

```c
int main() {
    char operator;
    float num1, num2;

    printf("Enter an operator (+, -, *, /): ");
    scanf(" %c", &operator);
    printf("Enter two numbers: ");
    scanf("%f %f", &num1, &num2);

    switch (operator) {
        case '+':
            printf("%.2f + %.2f = %.2f\n", num1, num2, num1 + num2);
            break;
        case '-':
            printf("%.2f - %.2f = %.2f\n", num1, num2, num1 - num2);
            break;
        case '*':
            printf("%.2f * %.2f = %.2f\n", num1, num2, num1 * num2);
            break;
        case '/':
            if (num2 != 0)
                printf("%.2f / %.2f = %.2f\n", num1, num2, num1 / num2);
            else
                printf("Error: Division by zero is not allowed.\n");
            break;
        default:
            printf("Invalid operator!\n");
    }

    return 0;
}
```

Output

Enter an operator (+, -, *, /): *
Enter two numbers: 5 3
5.00 * 3.00 = 15.00

The switch statement provides a clear and efficient way to handle multiple conditional branches based on a single variable or expression. It enhances readability and can simplify code compared to using multiple if-else statements, especially when dealing with a large number of conditions.

4.2.6 Nested Switch Statement
You can use one **switch** statement inside another **switch** statement(s). **nested switch case** is a switch statement that is placed inside another switch statement. This allows you to evaluate a second expression based on the value of the first switch case. It can be useful when you have multiple levels of conditions to check.

Syntax
```
switch (expression1) {
    case constant1:
        // Code to execute if expression1 == constant1
        switch (expression2) {
            case constantA:
                // Code for constantA
                break;
            case constantB:
                // Code for constantB
                break;
            // More cases as needed
            default:
                // Code if no case matches in the nested switch
        }
        break;
    case constant2:
        // Code for constant2
        break;
    // More cases as needed
    default:
        // Code if no case matches in the outer switch
}
```

Example 1: Grade Classification Based on Subject
In this example, we'll classify a student's grade based on their subject.
```
#include <stdio.h>
int main() {
    int subject;
    char grade;

    printf("Enter the subject (1: Math, 2: Science): ");
    scanf("%d", &subject);

    switch (subject) {
        case 1: // Math
            printf("Enter your grade (A, B, C, D, F): ");
```

```c
            scanf(" %c", &grade);
            switch (grade) {
                case 'A':
                    printf("Excellent in Math!\n");
                    break;
                case 'B':
                    printf("Good job in Math!\n");
                    break;
                case 'C':
                    printf("You passed in Math.\n");
                    break;
                case 'D':
                case 'F':
                    printf("You need to work harder in Math.\n");
                    break;
                default:
                    printf("Invalid grade for Math.\n");
            }
            break;

        case 2: // Science
            printf("Enter your grade (A, B, C, D, F): ");
            scanf(" %c", &grade);
            switch (grade) {
                case 'A':
                    printf("Excellent in Science!\n");
                    break;
                case 'B':
                    printf("Good job in Science!\n");
                    break;
                case 'C':
                    printf("You passed in Science.\n");
                    break;
                case 'D':
                case 'F':
                    printf("You need to work harder in Science.\n");
                    break;
                default:
                    printf("Invalid grade for Science.\n");
            }
            break;

        default:
```

```c
            printf("Invalid subject!\n");
    }

    return 0;
}
```
Output
Enter the subject (1: Math, 2: Science): 1
Enter your grade (A, B, C, D, F): B
Good job in Math!

Example 2: Menu Selection for Operations
In this example, we'll create a menu for different operations where the second menu is based on the selected operation type.

```c
#include <stdio.h>
int main() {
    int operation, type;

    printf("Select an operation:\n");
    printf("1. Arithmetic\n");
    printf("2. Logical\n");
    scanf("%d", &operation);

    switch (operation) {
        case 1: // Arithmetic
            printf("Select type:\n");
            printf("1. Addition\n");
            printf("2. Subtraction\n");
            scanf("%d", &type);
            switch (type) {
                case 1:
                    printf("You selected Addition.\n");
                    break;
                case 2:
                    printf("You selected Subtraction.\n");
                    break;
                default:
                    printf("Invalid type selected in Arithmetic.\n");
            }
            break;

        case 2: // Logical
            printf("Select type:\n");
            printf("1. AND\n");
            printf("2. OR\n");
```

```c
            scanf("%d", &type);
            switch (type) {
              case 1:
                 printf("You selected AND operation.\n");
                 break;
              case 2:
                 printf("You selected OR operation.\n");
                 break;
              default:
                 printf("Invalid type selected in Logical.\n");
            }
            break;

      default:
         printf("Invalid operation selected.\n");
   }

   return 0;
}
```

Output
Select an operation:
1. Arithmetic
2. Logical
2
Select type:
1. AND
2. OR
1
You selected AND operation.

A nested switch case allows for more complex decision-making by enabling multiple levels of conditional checks. This structure can simplify code when you need to handle various cases based on the outcomes of previous evaluations, making it a useful tool in C programming for organized control flow.

4.3 Loop Statements
A loop statement is used to execute a block of code repeatedly until a certain condition is true. It perform a certain operation repeatedly for finite number of times until condition is true

Let us X is an operation
#Perform X-Operation repeatedly until the condition is true

Examples
We will put our favorite song on a repeat mode until to get bored
Students write the exams until he completes all

4.3.1 For Loop
A **for loop** in C is a control flow statement that allows you to execute a block of code repeatedly for a specified number of iterations. It is commonly used when the number of iterations is known beforehand.

Flowchart of C Loop Statement
Given below is the general flowchart of a loop statement which is applicable to any programming language –

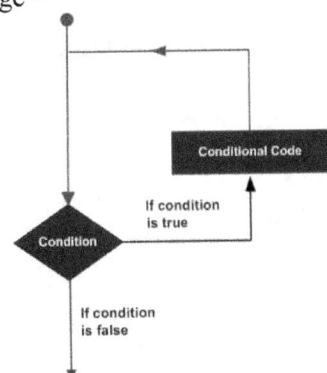

The statements in a C program are always executed in a top-to-bottom manner. If we ask the compiler to go back to any of the earlier steps, it constitutes a loop.

Syntax
for (initialization; condition; increment/decrement) {
    // Code to execute on each iteration
}
Components
1. **Initialization**: This is executed once at the beginning of the loop. It is typically used to declare and initialize a loop control variable.
2. **Condition**: This expression is evaluated before each iteration. If it is true, the loop continues; if false, the loop terminates.
3. **Increment/Decrement**: This is executed at the end of each iteration, usually to update the loop control variable.

Example 1: Print Numbers from 1 to 10
```c
#include <stdio.h>

int main() {
    int i;

    printf("Numbers from 1 to 10:\n");
    for (i = 1; i <= 10; i++) {
        printf("%d ", i);
    }
    printf("\n");

    return 0;
}
```
Output
Numbers from 1 to 10:
1 2 3 4 5 6 7 8 9 10

Example 2: Calculate the Sum of First N Natural Numbers
```c
#include <stdio.h>
int main() {
    int n, sum = 0;

    printf("Enter a positive integer: ");
    scanf("%d", &n);

    for (int i = 1; i <= n; i++) {
        sum += i; // Add i to sum
    }

    printf("The sum of the first %d natural numbers is %d.\n", n, sum);

    return 0;
}
```
Output
Enter a positive integer: 5
The sum of the first 5 natural numbers is 15.

Example 3: Print a Multiplication Table
```c
#include <stdio.h>
int main() {
    int number;

    printf("Enter a number to display its multiplication table: ");
    scanf("%d", &number);
```

```c
    printf("Multiplication table for %d:\n", number);
    for (int i = 1; i <= 10; i++) {
        printf("%d x %d = %d\n", number, i, number * i);
    }

    return 0;
}
```
Output
Enter a number to display its multiplication table: 3
Multiplication table for 3:
3 x 1 = 3
3 x 2 = 6
3 x 3 = 9
3 x 4 = 12
3 x 5 = 15
3 x 6 = 18
3 x 7 = 21
3 x 8 = 24
3 x 9 = 27
3 x 10 = 30

The for loop is a powerful and concise way to perform repetitive tasks in C programming. It is especially useful when you know in advance how many times you want to execute a statement or a block of code, making it a fundamental construct in the language.

4.3.2 While Loop

A **while loop** in C is a control flow statement that allows you to execute a block of code repeatedly as long as a specified condition is true. It is useful when the number of iterations is not known beforehand and depends on dynamic conditions.

Flowchart of C while Loop

The following flowchart represents how the **while** loop works –

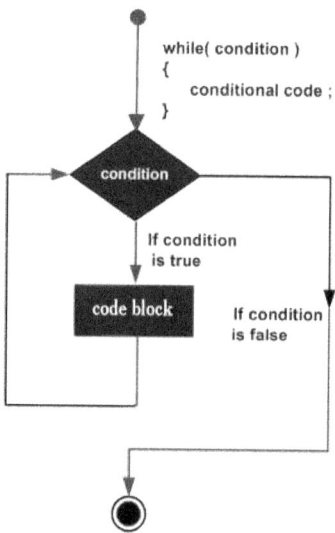

Syntax
while (condition) {
    // Code to execute while condition is true
}
Components
- **Condition**: This expression is evaluated before each iteration. If it evaluates to true, the loop continues; if false, the loop terminates.
- **Code Block**: This is the code that gets executed as long as the condition is true.

Example 1: Print Numbers from 1 to 10
include <stdio.h>

```
int main() {
    int i = 1; // Initialize the counter

    printf("Numbers from 1 to 10:\n");
    while (i <= 10) {
        printf("%d ", i);
        i++; // Increment the counter
    }
    printf("\n");

    return 0;
}
```
Output
Numbers from 1 to 10:

1 2 3 4 5 6 7 8 9 10

Example 2: Calculate the Sum of First N Natural Numbers

```c
#include <stdio.h>
int main() {
    int n, sum = 0, i = 1;

    printf("Enter a positive integer: ");
    scanf("%d", &n);

    while (i <= n) {
        sum += i; // Add i to sum
        i++; // Increment the counter
    }

    printf("The sum of the first %d natural numbers is %d.\n", n, sum);

    return 0;
}
```

Output
Enter a positive integer: 5
The sum of the first 5 natural numbers is 15.

Example 3: Reverse a Number

```c
#include <stdio.h>
int main() {
    int number, reversed = 0;

    printf("Enter an integer: ");
    scanf("%d", &number);

    while (number != 0) {
        int digit = number % 10; // Get the last digit
        reversed = reversed * 10 + digit; // Build the reversed number
        number /= 10; // Remove the last digit
    }

    printf("Reversed Number: %d\n", reversed);

    return 0;
}
```

Output
Enter an integer: 12345
Reversed Number: 54321

The while loop is a fundamental control structure in C that allows for executing a block of code repeatedly based on a condition. It is particularly useful when the number of iterations is not predetermined, giving programmers flexibility in how they manage loops in their code.

NOTE: Nested For Loop in C
A nested for loop is a loop inside another loop. This allows you to perform more complex iterations, often used for working with multi-dimensional data structures, such as arrays or matrices.

Syntax:
```
for (initialization1; condition1; increment/decrement1) {
    // Outer loop code

    for (initialization2; condition2; increment/decrement2) {
        // Inner loop code
    }
}
```

Explanation of Components
1. **Outer Loop**:
    - **Initialization1**: Sets up the loop control variable for the outer loop.
    - **Condition1**: The loop continues as long as this condition is true.
    - **Increment/Decrement1**: Updates the outer loop control variable after each iteration.
2. **Inner Loop**:
    - **Initialization2**: Sets up the loop control variable for the inner loop.
    - **Condition2**: The inner loop continues as long as this condition is true.
    - **Increment/Decrement2**: Updates the inner loop control variable after each iteration.

Example of Nested For Loop: Multiplication Table
```
#include <stdio.h>
int main() {
    int i, j;

    printf("Multiplication Table:\n");
    for (i = 1; i <= 10; i++) {
        for (j = 1; j <= 10; j++) {
            printf("%d x %d = %d\t", i, j, i * j);
        }
        printf("\n"); // New line after each row
    }
```

    return 0;
}
NOTE: Nested while loop
A nested while loop is a while loop placed inside another while loop. This allows you to perform more complex iterations, especially useful for handling multi-dimensional data or when you need to evaluate multiple conditions.
Syntax
while (condition1) {
    // Code to execute while condition1 is true

    while (condition2) {
        // Code to execute while condition2 is true
    }
}
Explanation of Components
1. **Outer While Loop**:
    - **Condition1**: The outer loop continues as long as this condition is true.
    - **Code Block**: This code executes for each iteration of the outer loop.
2. **Inner While Loop**:
    - **Condition2**: The inner loop continues as long as this condition is true.
    - **Code Block**: This code executes for each iteration of the inner loop for every iteration of the outer loop.

Example of Nested While Loop: Print a Multiplication Table

```c
#include <stdio.h>

int main() {
    int i = 1, j;

    printf("Multiplication Table:\n");
    while (i <= 10) { // Outer loop for the first number
        j = 1; // Reset j for each new i
        while (j <= 10) { // Inner loop for the second number
            printf("%d x %d = %d\t", i, j, i * j);
            j++; // Increment inner loop counter
        }
        printf("\n"); // New line after each row
        i++; // Increment outer loop counter
    }
```

    return 0;
}

4.3.3 Do-while Loop

A **do-while loop** in C is a control flow statement that allows you to execute a block of code repeatedly until a specified condition becomes false. The key feature of a do-while loop is that the code block is executed at least once, even if the condition is false from the start.

Flowchart of do while Loop

The following flowchart represents how the do-while loop works –

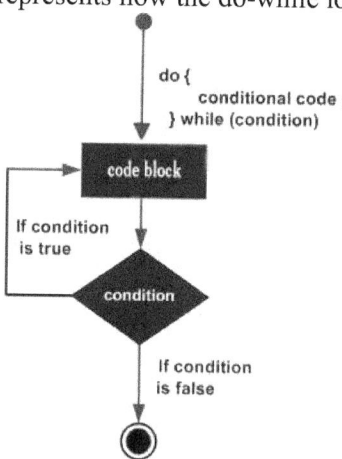

Since the expression that controls the loop is tested after the program runs the looping block for the first time, the do-while loop is called an "exit-verified loop". Here, the key point to note is that a do-while loop makes sure that the loop gets executed at least once.

Syntax

do {
    // Code to execute
} while (condition);

Components
- **Code Block**: The code inside the do block is executed first.
- **Condition**: After executing the block, the condition is evaluated. If it is true, the loop continues; if false, the loop terminates.

Example: Print Numbers from 1 to 10

#include <stdio.h>

int main() {
    int i = 1; // Initialize the counter

    printf("Numbers from 1 to 10:\n");

```c
    do {
        printf("%d ", i);
        i++; // Increment the counter
    } while (i <= 10);
    printf("\n");

    return 0;
}
```
Output
Numbers from 1 to 10:
1 2 3 4 5 6 7 8 9 10

Example 2: User Input with Validation
```c
#include <stdio.h>

int main() {
    int number;

    do {
        printf("Enter a positive integer: ");
        scanf("%d", &number);
    } while (number <= 0); // Repeat until a positive number is entered

    printf("You entered: %d\n", number);

    return 0;
}
```
Output
Enter a positive integer: -5
Enter a positive integer: 0
Enter a positive integer: 10
You entered: 10

Example 3: Calculate Factorial
```c
#include <stdio.h>

int main() {
    int number, factorial = 1;

    printf("Enter a positive integer: ");
    scanf("%d", &number);

    if (number < 0) {
        printf("Factorial is not defined for negative numbers.\n");
    } else {
```

```c
    int i = 1;
    do {
        factorial *= i; // Multiply factorial by i
        i++; // Increment the counter
    } while (i <= number);
    printf("Factorial of %d is %d.\n", number, factorial);
}

    return 0;
}
```

Output

Enter a positive integer: 5
Factorial of 5 is 120.

The do-while loop is a useful control structure in C that ensures a block of code is executed at least once before checking the condition. This makes it particularly suitable for scenarios where you want to prompt the user for input or ensure that certain operations occur before evaluating conditions.

NOTE: Nested Do-While Loop in C

A **nested do-while loop** is a do-while loop placed inside another do-while loop. This structure allows for complex iterations where you need to evaluate multiple conditions, ensuring that the inner loop executes at least once for each iteration of the outer loop.

Syntax

```
do {
    // Code to execute for the outer loop

    do {
        // Code to execute for the inner loop
    } while (condition2);

} while (condition1);
```

Explanation of Components
1. **Outer Do-While Loop**:
    o The code inside the outer do block is executed first.
    o After executing, it checks condition1. If true, it repeats; if false, it exits.
2. **Inner Do-While Loop**:
    o The code inside the inner do block executes at least once.
    o After executing, it checks condition2. If true, it repeats; if false, it exits.

Example of Nested Do-While Loop:Multiplication Table

an example of using nested do-while loops to print a multiplication table:

```c
#include <stdio.h>

int main() {
    int i = 1, j;

    printf("Multiplication Table:\n");
    do {
        j = 1; // Reset inner counter for each new value of i
        do {
            printf("%d x %d = %d\t", i, j, i * j);
            j++; // Increment inner loop counter
        } while (j <= 10); // Inner loop condition

        printf("\n"); // New line after each row
        i++; // Increment outer loop counter
    } while (i <= 10); // Outer loop condition

    return 0;
}
```

4.2.4 Nested Loops

Nested loops are loops placed inside another loop. This structure allows for more complex iterations, making it possible to handle multi-dimensional data structures, perform operations that depend on multiple conditions, or generate patterns.

When a looping construct in C is employed inside the body of another loop, we call it a **nested loop** (or, loops within a loop). Where, the loop that encloses the other loop is called the **outer loop**. The one that is enclosed is called the **inner loop**.

General Syntax of Nested Loops

The general form of a nested loop is as follows –

```
Outer loop {
    Inner loop {
        ...
        ...
    }
    ...
}
```

C provides three keywords for loops formation – while, do-while, and for. Nesting can be done on any of these three types of loops. That means you can put a while loop inside a for loop, a for loop inside a do-while loop, or any other combination.

Example 1: Printing a Multiplication Table

Here's an example of nested for loops to print a multiplication table.

```c
#include <stdio.h>

int main() {
    int i, j;

    printf("Multiplication Table:\n");
    for (i = 1; i <= 10; i++) { // Outer loop for the first number
        for (j = 1; j <= 10; j++) { // Inner loop for the second number
            printf("%d x %d = %d\t", i, j, i * j);
        }
        printf("\n"); // New line after each row
    }

    return 0;
}
```
Output
Multiplication Table:
Example 2: Pattern Generation
Here's another example where we create a simple pattern of asterisks using nested for loops.
```c
#include <stdio.h>

int main() {
    int rows, i, j;

    printf("Enter number of rows: ");
    scanf("%d", &rows);

    for (i = 1; i <= rows; i++) { // Outer loop for each row
        for (j = 1; j <= i; j++) { // Inner loop for printing stars
            printf("* ");
        }
        printf("\n"); // New line after each row
    }

    return 0;
}
```
Output (for 5 rows)
Enter number of rows: 5
*
* *
* * *
* * * *

* * * * *
Example 3: Summing Elements in a 2D Array
This example demonstrates how to sum elements in a two-dimensional array using nested loops.

```c
#include <stdio.h>

int main() {
    int rows = 3, cols = 3;
    int matrix[3][3] = {
        {1, 2, 3},
        {4, 5, 6},
        {7, 8, 9}
    };
    int sum = 0;

    // Nested loops to iterate through the matrix
    for (int i = 0; i < rows; i++) {
        for (int j = 0; j < cols; j++) {
            sum += matrix[i][j]; // Sum elements
        }
    }

    printf("Sum of all elements: %d\n", sum);

    return 0;
}
```
Output
Sum of all elements: 45

Nested loops are a powerful construct in C that enable you to handle complex scenarios involving multiple levels of iteration. They can be used for various applications, such as generating patterns, processing multi-dimensional arrays, and more. The flexibility of nested loops allows for a wide range of programming solutions

CHAPTER 5: FUNCTIONS

5.1 Functions Introduction

The Purpose of Function Concept in any Programming language is that "To Perform Certain Operation and Provides Code Re-Usability".

A function in C is a block of organized reusuable code that is performs a single related action. Every C program has at least one function, which is **main()**, and all the most trivial programs can define additional functions. A part of main program is called Function (OR) Sub Program of main program is called Function.

5.1.1 Why Functions

Functions are an essential feature of C programming for several reasons. Here are the key advantages of using functions:

1. **Modularity**:
   - Functions help break down complex programs into smaller, manageable sections or modules. Each function can handle a specific task, making it easier to develop, test, and maintain.
2. **Reusability**:
   - Once a function is defined, it can be called multiple times throughout the program. This reduces code duplication and saves development time. For instance, a sorting function can be reused in different parts of the program.
3. **Improved Readability**:
   - Functions can give descriptive names to blocks of code, making the program easier to read and understand. This is especially helpful for other programmers (or yourself) who might work on the code later.
4. **Ease of Maintenance**:
   - If a specific task needs to be modified, you only need to change the code in one place (inside the function) rather than throughout the entire program. This makes debugging and updates more straightforward.
5. **Abstraction**:
   - Functions allow programmers to hide complex logic behind a simple interface. Users can call a function without needing to understand its internal workings, promoting encapsulation.
6. **Namespace Management**:
   - Functions help manage the namespace in larger programs. By grouping related functionalities within functions, you can avoid variable name conflicts.
7. **Parameterization**:

- Functions can take parameters, allowing you to pass different data values to the same function. This flexibility lets you use the same function to handle various inputs.

8. **Recursion**:
    - Functions can call themselves (recursion), enabling elegant solutions for certain problems, such as tree traversals and factorial calculations.

Using functions in C programming is crucial for developing organized, maintainable, and efficient code. They enhance modularity, readability, and reusability, making programming easier and more effective. Understanding how to use functions is fundamental to becoming a proficient C programmer.

Types of Languages

In the context of Functions, we can classify the Programming languages into two types. They are

        a) Un-Structured Programming Languages
        b) Structured Programming Languages

a) Un-Structured Programming Languages:
=>In Un-Structured Programming Languages, we don't have the concept of Functions.
Example:- GW-BASIC
Since Un- Un-Structured Programming Languages does not contain Functions concept and It has the following Limitations.

        1. Application development time is More
        2. Application Takes More Memory Space.
        3. Application Excution time is more
        4. Application Performnace is degraded.
        5. Redundency (Duplication) of the the code.

b) Structured Programming Languages:
In Structured Programming Languages, we have the concept of Functions.
Example:- C,CPP,JAVA,PYTHON,.NET....etc
Since Structured Programming Languages contains Functions concept and It has the following Advantages.

        1. Application development time is Less
        2. Application Takes Less Memory Space.
        3. Application Excution time is Less.
        4. Application Performnace is Enhanced(Improved).
        5. Redundency (Duplication) of the the Minimized.

5.1.2 Types of Functions in C
We have two types of Functions. They are
   a) Pre-defined (or) Built-in Functions.
   b) Programmer / User / Custom Defined Functions.

Pre-defined (or) Built-in Functions:
These are also called as Standard Library Functions. Pre-defined (or) Built-in Functions are those which are already developed and available in C API and They re-used by C Programmers for dealing with Unversal Purpose.
Examples include:
- **Input/Output Functions**: printf(), scanf()
- **String Functions**: strlen(), strcpy(), strcat()
- **Mathematical Functions**: sqrt(), pow(), sin()

Programmer / User / Custom Defined Functions:
Programmer / User / Custom Defined Functions are developed by Python Programmers and re-used by other Python programmers and they are meant for performing common operations.
Examples:
   deposit()
   withdraw()
   balenq()
   genotp()...etc

5.1.3 Parts of a Function in C
A function in C consists of several key components. Understanding these components is crucial for effectively defining and using functions in your programs.

```
1  int a = 10, b = 5, c;
2
3  int product(int x, int y);        — Function Prototype   — int is the return type and int x and int y are
4                                                             the function arguments
5  int main(void)
6  {                                 — Main Function        — int is always the return type and there are no
7      c = product(a,b);                                      arguments, hence the (void). Curly braces
8                                                             {} mark the start and end of the main
9      printf("%i\n",c);                                      function
10                                   — Function call        — product(a,b); a and b are global variables the
11     return 0;                                              function is passed. Here the values returned
12 }                                                          by the function are assigned to the variable
13                                                            c
14 int product(int x, int y)         — Function Definition  — contains the function statement return(x * y);
15 {                                                          the function returns x times y to the main
16     return (x * y);                                        function where it was called. Curly braces {}
17 }                                                          mark the start and end of the function
```

94

- **Function Declaration (Prototype)**

The function declaration specifies the function's name, return type, and parameters (if any). It informs the compiler about the function's existence before it is called in the code.

Syntax

return_type function_name(parameter_type parameter_name);

Example

int add(int a, int b);

Explanation
- **int**: This indicates that the function returns an integer value.
- **add**: This is the name of the function.
- **int a, int b**: These are the parameters of the function, which are also of type integer.

- **Function Definition**

The function definition provides the actual implementation of the function. It includes the return type, name, parameters, and the body of the function, which contains the code to be executed.

Syntax

return_type function_name(parameter_type parameter_name) {
 // Function body
 // Code to execute
}

Example

int add(int a, int b) {
 return a + b; // Return the sum of a and b
}

Explanation
- The function add takes two integer parameters a and b.
- Inside the function body, the sum of a and b is calculated and returned.

- **Function Call**

A function call is the point in the program where the function is executed. When a function is called, the control of the program transfers to that function.

Syntax

function_name(argument1, argument2);

Example

int main() {
  int result;
  result = add(5, 10); // Function call
  printf("Sum: %d\n", result);
  return 0;
}

Explanation
- The function add is called with arguments 5 and 10.

- The result of the function (which is 15) is stored in the variable result.
- The printf statement outputs the sum.

Complete Example

Here's a complete example demonstrating all components:

```
#include <stdio.h>

// Function declaration
int add(int a, int b);

int main() {
    int result;
    // Function call
    result = add(5, 10);
    printf("Sum: %d\n", result); // Output the result
    return 0;
}

// Function definition
int add(int a, int b) {
    return a + b; // Return the sum of a and b
}
```

Output

Sum: 15

A function in C comprises three main components: the function declaration (prototype), the function definition, and the function call. Understanding these components is essential for creating and using functions effectively, allowing for modular programming and improved code organization.

5.1.4 Function definition and declaration

In C programming, **function declaration** and **function definition** are two distinct concepts that play critical roles in how functions are used. Let's explore each one.

Function Declaration

Definition: A function declaration (also known as a function prototype) introduces a function's name, return type, and parameters to the compiler. It informs the compiler about the function's characteristics before its actual implementation appears in the code.

Syntax

return_type function_name(parameter_type parameter_name);

Example

int add(int a, int b);

Explanation

- **Return Type**: int indicates that the function returns an integer value.

- **Function Name**: add is the name of the function.
- **Parameters**: The function takes two parameters, both of type int.

Function declarations are usually placed at the beginning of a source file or in header files, allowing the compiler to recognize calls to the function even if the definition appears later.

Function Definition

Definition: A function definition provides the actual implementation of the function. It includes the return type, function name, parameters, and the body of the function, which contains the executable code.

Syntax

```
return_type function_name(parameter_type parameter_name) {
    // Function body
    // Code to execute
}
```

Example

```
int add(int a, int b) {
    return a + b; // Return the sum of a and b
}
```

Explanation
- The function add takes two integer parameters, a and b.
- The function body contains the logic to compute the sum and return it.

Complete Example

Here's how both concepts work together in a program:

```
#include <stdio.h>

// Function declaration
int add(int a, int b);

int main() {
    int result;
    // Function call
    result = add(5, 10);
    printf("Sum: %d\n", result); // Output the result
    return 0;
}

// Function definition
int add(int a, int b) {
    return a + b; // Return the sum of a and b
}
```

Output

Sum: 15

Summary

- **Function Declaration**: Introduces the function to the compiler, specifying its return type, name, and parameters without providing the body. It allows for early use of the function in the code.
- **Function Definition**: Provides the complete implementation of the function, including the body where the logic resides.

Understanding the difference between declaration and definition is crucial for proper function usage in C programming.

5.1.5 Function Arguments and Return Values
Parameter:
A parameter is a variable that is used in a function definition to receive values passed to that function when it is called. Parameters allow functions to operate on input data, making them versatile and reusable.

Types of Parameters
   (a) **Formal Parameters:** These are the parameters defined in the function declaration/definition. They act as placeholders for the actual values (arguments) that will be passed when the function is called.
   (b) **Actual Parameters (Arguments):** These are the actual values you pass to the function when calling it.

Syntax

The syntax for defining parameters in a function is as follows:

```
return_type function_name(parameter_type parameter_name) {
    // Function body
}
```

Example 1: Basic Function with Parameters

Here's a simple example demonstrating how parameters work in a function.

```c
#include <stdio.h>

// Function declaration with parameters
void printSum(int a, int b) {
    int sum = a + b; // Use parameters a and b
    printf("Sum: %d\n", sum);
}

int main() {
    // Calling the function with actual parameters
    printSum(5, 10); // Here, 5 and 10 are actual parameters
    return 0;
}
```

Explanation
- **Function Definition**: void printSum(int a, int b) defines a function printSum with two parameters, a and b, both of type int.

- **Function Call**: printSum(5, 10) calls the function and passes the values 5 and 10 as actual parameters.
- The function calculates the sum of a and b and prints it.

Example 2: Function with Multiple Parameter Types

Here's another example demonstrating a function with different parameter types.

```
#include <stdio.h>

// Function that takes multiple parameter types
void displayInfo(char name[], int age) {
    printf("Name: %s, Age: %d\n", name, age);
}

int main() {
    // Calling the function with actual parameters
    displayInfo("Alice", 30); // "Alice" is a string argument, 30 is an integer argument
    return 0;
}
```

Explanation

- **Function Definition**: void displayInfo(char name[], int age) takes a string (character array) and an integer as parameters.
- **Function Call**: displayInfo("Alice", 30) passes the string "Alice" and the integer 30 to the function.
- The function prints the provided name and age.
- **Summary**
- **Parameters** are essential for making functions flexible and reusable, allowing them to work with various inputs.
- They act as placeholders for values that are passed during a function call, enabling the function to process those values as needed.

Understanding how to use parameters effectively is crucial for writing modular and maintainable C programs.

5.1.6 Scope and Lifetime of Variables

Variable:

A **variable** in C programming is a named storage location in memory that can hold a value. The value stored in a variable can change during program execution. Variables are fundamental to programming because they allow you to store and manipulate data.

Characteristics of Variables

1. **Name**: Each variable has a unique name (identifier) that you use to refer to it in your program. Variable names must follow specific

naming rules (e.g., they cannot start with a digit, and cannot contain spaces).
2. **Data Type**: Each variable has a data type, which determines the kind of data it can hold (e.g., integers, floating-point numbers, characters). The data type also defines how much memory the variable occupies.
3. **Value**: The value is the data stored in the variable. You can change this value as the program runs.
4. **Memory Location**: Variables occupy a specific location in memory, which is used to store the value.

Declaring Variables
Before using a variable, you must declare it, specifying its name and data type.
Syntax
data_type variable_name;
Example
int age;   // Declares an integer variable named age
float salary;   // Declares a float variable named salary
char grade;   // Declares a character variable named grade

Initializing Variables
You can also assign an initial value to a variable when you declare it.
Example
int age = 25;   // Initializes age with the value 25
float salary = 50000.50; // Initializes salary with the value 50000.50
char grade = 'A';   // Initializes grade with the character 'A'

Using Variables
Once declared and initialized, you can use variables in expressions and statements.
Example

```
#include <stdio.h>

int main() {
    int age = 25;            // Declare and initialize a variable
    float salary = 50000.50; // Another variable

    // Outputting variable values
    printf("Age: %d\n", age);
    printf("Salary: %.2f\n", salary);

    // Changing the value of the variable
    age = 30; // Updating age
    printf("Updated Age: %d\n", age);

    return 0;
}
```

Output
Age: 25
Salary: 50000.50
Updated Age: 30

5.1.7 Types of Variables
In C programming, variables can be classified based on their **scope** and **lifetime**. The two primary types are **local variables** and **global variables**. Here's a detailed explanation of both types:

(a) Local Variables
Definition: Local variables are declared within a function or a block (enclosed by curly braces {}). They are accessible only within that function or block, and their lifetime is limited to the duration of that function or block.

Characteristics
- **Scope**: Limited to the function or block in which they are declared.
- **Lifetime**: Created when the function is called and destroyed when the function exits.
- **Initialization**: Local variables may contain garbage values if not explicitly initialized.

Example
```
#include <stdio.h>

void display() {
    int localVar = 5; // Local variable
    printf("Local Variable: %d\n", localVar);
}

int main() {
    display();
    // printf("%d", localVar); // Error: localVar is not accessible here
    return 0;
}
```
Output
Local Variable: 5

(b) Global Variables
Definition: Global variables are declared outside of any function. They can be accessed by any function within the same file (or even other files if declared appropriately). Their lifetime extends throughout the program's execution.

Characteristics
- **Scope**: Accessible from any function in the program after its declaration.
- **Lifetime**: Created when the program starts and destroyed when the program ends.

- **Initialization**: Global variables are automatically initialized to zero if not explicitly initialized.

Example

```
#include <stdio.h>

int globalVar = 10; // Global variable

void display() {
   printf("Global Variable: %d\n", globalVar);
}

int main() {
   display(); // Accessing global variable
   globalVar = 20; // Modifying global variable
   printf("Modified Global Variable: %d\n", globalVar);
   return 0;
}
```

Output

Global Variable: 10
Modified Global Variable: 20

Summary
- **Local Variables**:
    - Declared within a function or block.
    - Scope is limited to that function/block.
    - Created and destroyed during the function's execution.
- **Global Variables**:
    - Declared outside any function.
    - Accessible from any function in the file.
    - Created at program startup and destroyed at program termination.

Understanding the differences between local and global variables is crucial for managing variable scope and avoiding naming conflicts in larger programs.

5.1.8 Recursive Functions

A **recursive function** is a function that calls itself in order to solve a problem. This approach allows complex problems to be broken down into smaller, more manageable subproblems.

Recursive functions typically consist of two key components: a **base case** and a **recursive case**.

- **Base Case**: A condition that stops the recursion when met. It prevents infinite recursion.
- **Recursive Case**: The part of the function that includes the recursive call to itself with modified arguments.
- **Syntax of a Recursive Function**

The syntax of a recursive function follows the general format of a function declaration in C:

```
return_type function_name(parameters) {
    // Base case
    if (base_condition) {
        return base_value; // Return when base case is met
    }
    // Recursive case
    return function_name(modified_parameters); // Call itself
}
```

Example 1: Calculating Factorial

The factorial of a non-negative integer n is defined as:
- n!=n×(n−1)!
- Base case: 0!=1

Program:

```c
#include <stdio.h>

// Recursive function to calculate factorial
int factorial(int n) {
    // Base case
    if (n == 0) {
        return 1; // 0! is 1
    }
    // Recursive case
    return n * factorial(n - 1); // n! = n * (n-1)!
}

int main() {
    int num = 5; // Input value
    printf("Factorial of %d is %d\n", num, factorial(num)); // Function call
    return 0;
}
```

Explanation
1. **Function Definition**: factorial(int n) is a recursive function that calculates the factorial of n.
2. **Base Case**: When n is 0, it returns 1.
3. **Recursive Case**: For any other positive integer n, it returns n multiplied by the factorial of n-1.
4. **Main Function**: Calls the factorial function with the input 5 and prints the result.

Output
Factorial of 5 is 120

Example 2: Fibonacci Series
The Fibonacci sequence is defined as:
- $F(0)=0$
- $F(1)=1$
- $F(n)=F(n-1)+F(n-2)$ for $n \geq 2$

Program:
```c
#include <stdio.h>

// Recursive function to calculate Fibonacci
int fibonacci(int n) {
    // Base cases
    if (n == 0) {
        return 0; // F(0) = 0
    } else if (n == 1) {
        return 1; // F(1) = 1
    }
    // Recursive case
    return fibonacci(n - 1) + fibonacci(n - 2); // F(n) = F(n-1) + F(n-2)
}

int main() {
    int num = 6; // Input value
    printf("Fibonacci of %d is %d\n", num, fibonacci(num)); // Function call
    return 0;
}
```

Explanation
1. **Function Definition**: fibonacci(int n) is a recursive function that calculates the nnn-th Fibonacci number.
2. **Base Cases**: Returns 0 for F(0) and 1 for F(1).
3. **Recursive Case**: For other values of n, it calls itself to compute the sum of the two preceding Fibonacci numbers.
4. **Main Function**: Calls the fibonacci function with the input 6 and prints the result.

Output
Fibonacci of 6 is 8

Summary
- **Recursive Functions**: Solve problems by calling themselves with smaller inputs.
- **Base Case**: Prevents infinite recursion by specifying conditions under which the function will stop calling itself.
- **Recursive Case**: Contains the logic to call the function with modified arguments.

Recursive functions are powerful tools for solving problems, but they should be used carefully to avoid excessive resource consumption and potential stack overflow errors.
4o mini

5.1.9 Inline Functions

An **inline function** is a function that is expanded in line when it is called, rather than being invoked through the standard function call mechanism. This means that instead of generating a function call, the compiler replaces the call with the actual function code. The main purpose of inline functions is to reduce the overhead associated with function calls, especially for small, frequently called functions.

Advantages of Inline Functions
1. **Performance Improvement**: Inline functions can improve performance by eliminating the overhead of function calls.
2. **Reduced Function Call Overhead**: Since inline functions are expanded at the point of invocation, there's no need to push arguments onto the stack or pop them off.
3. **Code Clarity**: They can make code cleaner and easier to read, especially for simple operations.

- **Syntax of Inline Functions**

To define an inline function, you can use the inline keyword before the return type in the function definition:

```
inline return_type function_name(parameters) {
    // function body
}
```

Example Program: Inline Function
Here's a simple example demonstrating the use of an inline function to calculate the square of a number.

Program:
```
#include <stdio.h>

// Inline function to calculate square
inline int square(int x) {
    return x * x; // Returns the square of x
}

int main() {
    int num = 5;
    printf("The square of %d is %d\n", num, square(num)); // Function call
    return 0;
}
```

Explanation
1. **Inline Function Definition**:

        ○ The function square is defined with the inline keyword.
        ○ It takes an integer parameter x and returns its square.
   2. **Function Call**:
        ○ In the main function, square(num) is called. The compiler replaces this call with the expression num * num during compilation.
   3. **Output**:
        ○ The program calculates the square of 5 and prints the result.

Output
The square of 5 is 25

Important Considerations
   1. **Compiler's Discretion**: The compiler may ignore the inline keyword and choose not to inline a function, especially if it is too complex or if optimization settings do not allow it.
   2. **Code Bloat**: Excessive use of inline functions can lead to code bloat (larger binary size), as the function code is duplicated at each point of call.
   3. **Debugging**: Inline functions can make debugging more challenging since the function calls are replaced with code.

Summary
Inline functions are a useful feature in C that can improve performance by reducing the overhead of function calls. By using the inline keyword, you can define small functions that are expanded at the point of invocation, leading to potentially faster execution. However, they should be used judiciously to avoid issues such as code bloat and complexity in debugging.

5.1.10 Storage Classes

In C programming, a **storage class** defines the scope (visibility), lifetime, and storage location of a variable. There are four primary storage classes in C:
   1. **Automatic Storage Class** (auto)
   2. **Static Storage Class** (static)
   3. **Register Storage Class** (register)
   4. **External Storage Class** (extern)

Let's explore each of these storage classes in detail, along with example programs.

1. Automatic Storage Class (auto)
   - **Scope**: Local to the block in which it is declared.
   - **Lifetime**: Exists only during the execution of the block.
   - **Default**: Variables declared inside a function are automatically considered as auto.

Example:
#include <stdio.h>

void function() {

```
    auto int a = 10; // 'auto' is optional
    printf("Inside function: %d\n", a);
}

int main() {
    function();
    // printf("%d", a); // Error: 'a' is not accessible here
    return 0;
}
```
Output
Inside function: 10

2. Static Storage Class (static)
- **Scope**: Local to the function or file in which it is declared.
- **Lifetime**: Exists for the entire duration of the program.
- **Initialization**: Static variables are initialized only once, and retain their value between function calls.

Example:
```
#include <stdio.h>

void counter() {
    static int count = 0; // Static variable
    count++;
    printf("Count: %d\n", count);
}

int main() {
    for (int i = 0; i < 5; i++) {
        counter(); // Function calls
    }
    return 0;
}
```
Output
Count: 1
Count: 2
Count: 3
Count: 4
Count: 5

3. Register Storage Class (register)
- **Scope**: Local to the block in which it is declared.
- **Lifetime**: Exists only during the execution of the block.
- **Purpose**: Suggests to the compiler to store the variable in a CPU register for faster access. This is a hint, and the compiler may ignore it.

Example:

```c
#include <stdio.h>

int main() {
    register int i; // Request for register storage
    for (i = 0; i < 5; i++) {
        printf("%d ", i);
    }
    printf("\n");
    return 0;
}
```
Output
0 1 2 3 4

4. External Storage Class (extern)
- **Scope**: Global; can be accessed by any function within the same or different files.
- **Lifetime**: Exists for the entire duration of the program.
- **Purpose**: Declares a variable that is defined in another file or elsewhere in the same file.

Example:
```c
#include <stdio.h>

// External variable declaration
extern int globalVar; // Declaration

void display() {
    printf("Global Variable: %d\n", globalVar);
}

int globalVar = 100; // Definition

int main() {
    display(); // Function call
    return 0;
}
```
Output
Global Variable: 100

Summary of Storage Classes

Storage Class	Scope	Lifetime	Initialization
auto	Local to the block	Duration of the block	Automatic (garbage value)
static	Local to the function or file	Entire program duration	Initialized only once

register	Local to the block	Duration of the block	Automatic (garbage value)
extern	Global	Entire program duration	Static (initialized to 0)

Understanding storage classes in C is crucial for effective memory management and controlling variable scope and lifetime. Each storage class serves a specific purpose, and using them appropriately can lead to more efficient and maintainable code.

CHAPTER 6: ARRAYS

6.1 Arrays
6.1.1 Arrays Introduction
An **array** in C is a collection of elements of the same data type, stored in contiguous memory locations. Arrays allow you to store multiple values in a single variable, making it easier to manage and manipulate large sets of related data.

Characteristics of Arrays
1. **Fixed Size**: The size of an array must be specified at the time of declaration and cannot be changed during runtime.
2. **Homogeneous Data Types**: All elements in an array must be of the same type (e.g., all integers, all floats).
3. **Zero-Based Indexing**: Array indexing starts from 0. The first element is accessed using index 0, the second element using index 1, and so on.
4. **Memory Allocation**: Arrays are allocated in a single block of memory, which allows for efficient access to elements using their indices.

C array is beneficial if you have to store similar elements. For example, if we want to store the marks of a student in 6 subjects, then we don't need to define different variables for the marks in the different subject. Instead of that, we can define an array which can store the marks in each subject at the contiguous memory locations. By using the array, we can access the elements easily. Only a few lines of code are required to access the elements of the array.

Properties of Arrays
The array contains the following properties.
- Each element of an array is of same data type and carries the same size, i.e., int = 4 bytes.
- Elements of the array are stored at contiguous memory locations where the first element is stored at the smallest memory location.
- Elements of the array can be randomly accessed since we can calculate the address of each element of the array with the given base address and the size of the data element.

6.1.2 Why Use Arrays in C
Arrays are a fundamental data structure in C that provide several advantages for managing collections of data. Here are some key reasons to use arrays:
1. **Efficient Memory Management**:
    - Arrays allocate memory in contiguous blocks, which makes access to elements faster due to better cache locality.
    - This structure minimizes overhead associated with dynamic memory allocation and pointers.
2. **Easy Data Organization**:

- Arrays allow you to group related data under a single variable name, improving code organization and readability.
- For example, you can store a list of student scores in a single array instead of declaring multiple variables.

3. **Random Access**:
   - Arrays provide constant-time access (O(1) complexity) to elements using their index, making it easy to retrieve or modify data quickly.
   - This is particularly useful for applications requiring frequent read/write operations on a dataset.

4. **Simplified Looping**:
   - Arrays can be easily iterated over using loops, which simplifies processing collections of data.
   - This makes tasks like summing values, finding averages, or searching for elements straightforward.

5. **Supports Multidimensional Structures**:
   - Arrays can be multi-dimensional (e.g., 2D arrays), which allows you to represent matrices, tables, or grids easily.
   - This is particularly useful in applications such as image processing, simulations, or mathematical computations.

6. **Static Size**:
   - Arrays have a fixed size determined at compile time, which can lead to optimizations in memory usage and allocation.
   - This predictability can be beneficial in embedded systems or applications where memory usage is critical.

7. **Foundation for Other Data Structures**:
   - Arrays serve as the underlying structure for more complex data structures like lists, stacks, queues, and even hash tables.
   - Understanding arrays is essential for grasping these advanced concepts.

Example Use Cases
- **Storing Grades**: For a program that processes student grades, an array can efficiently hold all the grades for easy access and computation.
- **Image Processing**: Images can be represented as 2D arrays, where each element corresponds to a pixel's color value.
- **Game Development**: Arrays can represent game boards, inventories, or configurations of game entities.

Advantage of C Array
1) **Code Optimization:** Less code to the access the data.
2) **Ease of traversing:** By using the for loop, we can retrieve the elements of an array easily.
3) **Ease of sorting**: To sort the elements of the array, we need a few lines of code only.

4) Random Access: We can access any element randomly using the array.
Disadvantage of C Array
1) Fixed Size: Whatever size, we define at the time of declaration of the array, we can't exceed the limit. So, it doesn't grow the size dynamically like LinkedList which we will learn later.
Summary
Arrays are a powerful tool in C for organizing, managing, and processing collections of data. Their efficiency, simplicity, and flexibility make them an essential feature for many programming tasks. Whether you're handling numerical data, text, or more complex structures, understanding and utilizing arrays can greatly enhance your programming capabilities.

6.2 Types of Arrays in C
In C, arrays can be categorized based on their dimensions

6.2.1 One-Dimensional Arrays
A **one-dimensional array** is a linear data structure that stores a fixed-size sequence of elements, all of the same data type. You can think of it as a list or a row of elements, where each element can be accessed using a single index.
Characteristics of One-Dimensional Arrays
1. **Contiguous Memory Allocation**: All elements are stored in contiguous memory locations, which allows for efficient access and manipulation.
2. **Fixed Size**: The size of the array must be defined at the time of declaration and cannot be changed later.
3. **Homogeneous Data Type**: All elements in a one-dimensional array must be of the same type (e.g., all integers, all floats).
4. **Zero-Based Indexing**: The first element is accessed using index 0, the second element with index 1, and so on.

A one-dimensional array can be viewed as a linear sequence of elements. We can only increase or decrease its size in a single direction. Only a single row exists in the one-dimensional array and every element within the array is accessible by the index. In C, array indexing starts zero-indexing i.e. the first element is at index 0, the second at index 1, and so on up to n-1 for an array of size n.

One Dimensional Array in C

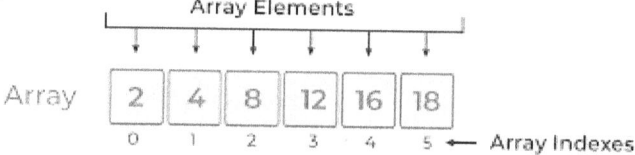

1-D Array Declaration:
In C, a one-dimensional array is declared by specifying the data type, the name of the array, and the size of the array in square brackets. Here's the general syntax for declaring a one-dimensional array:
   data_type array_name[size];
- **data_type**: This specifies the type of data the array will hold (e.g., int, float, char).
- **array_name**: This is the identifier you choose for the array.
- **size**: This indicates the number of elements the array can hold, and it must be a positive integer.

Example of One-Dimensional Array Declaration
Here are a few examples of how to declare one-dimensional arrays:
1. **Integer Array**:
   int numbers[5]; // Declaration of an integer array with 5 elements
2. **Float Array**:
   float prices[10]; // Declaration of a float array with 10 elements
3. **Character Array**:
   char name[20]; // Declaration of a character array (can be used for strings)

To declare a one-dimensional array in C, you specify its data type, name, and size. You can also initialize the array at the time of declaration. Understanding how to declare and initialize arrays is fundamental for managing collections of data effectively in C programming.

1-D Array Initialization:
In C, initializing a one-dimensional array means assigning values to its elements at the time of declaration. This process can be done in several ways, and understanding these methods is essential for effective array management.

Basic Syntax for Initialization
The general syntax for initializing a one-dimensional array is as follows:
   data_type array_name[size] = {value1, value2, ..., valueN};

Examples of One-Dimensional Array Initialization
1. Integer Array Initialization
Example:
```
#include <stdio.h>

int main() {
   // Declaration and initialization of an integer array
   int numbers[5] = {10, 20, 30, 40, 50};

   // Printing the array elements
   printf("Integer Array Elements:\n");
   for (int i = 0; i < 5; i++) {
      printf("%d ", numbers[i]);
```

    }
    printf("\n");

    return 0;
}
Output:
Integer Array Elements:
10 20 30 40 50
2. Float Array Initialization
Example:
#include <stdio.h>

int main() {
    // Declaration and initialization of a float array
    float prices[3] = {9.99, 14.50, 7.25};

    // Printing the array elements
    printf("Float Array Elements:\n");
    for (int i = 0; i < 3; i++) {
        printf("%.2f ", prices[i]);
    }
    printf("\n");

    return 0;
}
Output:
Float Array Elements:
9.99 14.50 7.25
3. Character Array Initialization (String)
Example:
#include <stdio.h>

int main() {
    // Declaration and initialization of a character array (string)
    char greeting[6] = "Hello"; // The size includes space for the null terminator

    // Printing the string
    printf("Greeting: %s\n", greeting);

    return 0;
}
Output:
Greeting: Hello

1-D Array Elements Access:
Accessing elements in a one-dimensional array in C is straightforward. You use the array's name followed by an index in square brackets to refer to a specific element. The index is zero-based, meaning that the first element is at index 0, the second at index 1, and so on.

Syntax for Accessing Array Elements
To access an element of a one-dimensional array, you use the following syntax:
c
Copy code
array_name[index]
- **array_name**: The name of the array.
- **index**: The position of the element you want to access (starting from 0).
- **Example: Accessing Array Elements**

Here's a simple example that demonstrates how to declare an array, initialize it, and access its elements:

```c
#include <stdio.h>

int main() {
    // Declaration and initialization of an integer array
    int numbers[5] = {10, 20, 30, 40, 50};

    // Accessing and printing individual elements
    printf("First element: %d\n", numbers[0]);   // Accessing the first element
    printf("Second element: %d\n", numbers[1]);  // Accessing the second element
    printf("Third element: %d\n", numbers[2]);   // Accessing the third element
    printf("Fourth element: %d\n", numbers[3]);  // Accessing the fourth element
    printf("Fifth element: %d\n", numbers[4]);   // Accessing the fifth element

    return 0;
}
```

Output
yaml
Copy code
First element: 10
Second element: 20
Third element: 30
Fourth element: 40
Fifth element: 50

Modifying Array Elements

You can also modify the elements of an array by accessing them through their index. Here's an example that demonstrates how to change the value of specific elements:
#include <stdio.h>

```
int main() {
    // Declaration and initialization of an integer array
    int numbers[5] = {10, 20, 30, 40, 50};

    // Modifying the elements
    numbers[0] = 100; // Change first element to 100
    numbers[2] = 300; // Change third element to 300

    // Printing the modified array elements
    printf("Modified Array Elements:\n");
    for (int i = 0; i < 5; i++) {
        printf("%d ", numbers[i]); // Accessing and printing each element
    }
    printf("\n");

    return 0;
}
```

Output
Modified Array Elements:
100 20 300 40 50

Summary
- **Accessing Elements**: Use the array name followed by the index in square brackets to access individual elements.
- **Modifying Elements**: You can assign new values to specific elements using the same syntax.

Understanding how to access and modify elements in a one-dimensional array is crucial for effective data manipulation in C programming.

6.2.2 Two-Dimensional Arrays

A **two-dimensional array** in C is essentially an array of arrays. It can be visualized as a table or matrix with rows and columns. Each element in a two-dimensional array can be accessed using two indices: one for the row and one for the column.

Characteristics of Two-Dimensional Arrays
1. **Contiguous Memory Allocation**: Elements are stored in a contiguous block of memory.
2. **Fixed Size**: The size of the array must be defined at the time of declaration.

3. **Homogeneous Data Type**: All elements must be of the same data type.
4. **Zero-Based Indexing**: Indexing starts at 0, so the first element is accessed with indices [0][0].

A two-dimensional array in an array of one-dimensional arrays. Each element of a two-dimensional array is an array itself. It is like a table or a matrix. The elements can be considered to be logically arranged in rows and columns. Hence, the location of any element is characterised by its row number and column number. Both row and column index start from 0.

	Column 0	Column 1	Column 2	Column 3
Row 0	a[0][0]	a[0][1]	a[0][2]	a[0][3]
Row 1	a[1][0]	a[1][1]	a[1][2]	a[1][3]
Row 2	a[2][0]	a[2][1]	a[2][2]	a[2][3]

Syntax for Declaration
The syntax for declaring a two-dimensional array is:
data_type array_name[rows][columns];
- **data_type**: The type of data the array will hold (e.g., int, float, char).
- **array_name**: The name of the array.
- **rows**: The number of rows in the array.
- **columns**: The number of columns in the array.

Example: Declaration and Initialization
Here's an example of how to declare, initialize, and access elements in a two-dimensional array.

1. Declaration and Initialization
```
#include <stdio.h>

int main() {
    // Declaration and initialization of a 2D integer array (3 rows and 4 columns)
    int matrix[3][4] = {
        {1, 2, 3, 4},
        {5, 6, 7, 8},
        {9, 10, 11, 12}
    };

    // Printing the array elements
    printf("Matrix Elements:\n");
    for (int i = 0; i < 3; i++) {
        for (int j = 0; j < 4; j++) {
            printf("%d ", matrix[i][j]); // Accessing elements by row and column
        }
        printf("\n"); // New line for each row
```

    }
    return 0;
}
Output:
Matrix Elements:
1 2 3 4
5 6 7 8
9 10 11 12

2. Accessing and Modifying Elements
You can access and modify elements in a two-dimensional array using their row and column indices.

```c
#include <stdio.h>

int main() {
    // Declaration and initialization of a 2D integer array
    int matrix[3][3] = {
        {1, 2, 3},
        {4, 5, 6},
        {7, 8, 9}
    };

    // Accessing and printing specific elements
    printf("Element at (1, 1): %d\n", matrix[1][1]); // Accessing element at row 1, column 1 (5)

    // Modifying an element
    matrix[0][2] = 99; // Changing the element at (0, 2) from 3 to 99

    // Printing the modified array
    printf("Modified Matrix Elements:\n");
    for (int i = 0; i < 3; i++) {
        for (int j = 0; j < 3; j++) {
            printf("%d ", matrix[i][j]); // Accessing each element
        }
        printf("\n"); // New line for each row
    }

    return 0;
}
```

Output:
Element at (1, 1): 5
Modified Matrix Elements:

1 2 99
4 5 6
7 8 9

Summary

- **Two-Dimensional Array**: A matrix-like structure where elements are accessed using two indices (row and column).
- **Declaration**: data_type array_name[rows][columns];
- **Initialization**: Elements can be initialized at the time of declaration using nested braces.
- **Accessing Elements**: Use array_name[row_index][column_index] to access specific elements.

Understanding two-dimensional arrays is crucial for working with data in a structured format, such as matrices and grids, in C programming.

6.2.3 Multi-Dimensional Arrays

A **multi-dimensional array** in C is an array that contains more than two dimensions. It can be thought of as an array of arrays, where each element itself can be an array. The most common types of multi-dimensional arrays are two-dimensional arrays (matrices) and three-dimensional arrays.

- **Characteristics of Multi-Dimensional Arrays**
1. **Contiguous Memory Allocation**: All elements are stored in contiguous memory locations.
2. **Fixed Size**: The size of the array must be defined at the time of declaration.
3. **Homogeneous Data Type**: All elements must be of the same type.
4. **Zero-Based Indexing**: Indexing starts at 0.

A **Three-Dimensional Array** or **3D** array in C is a collection of two-dimensional arrays. It can be visualized as multiple 2D arrays stacked on top of each other.

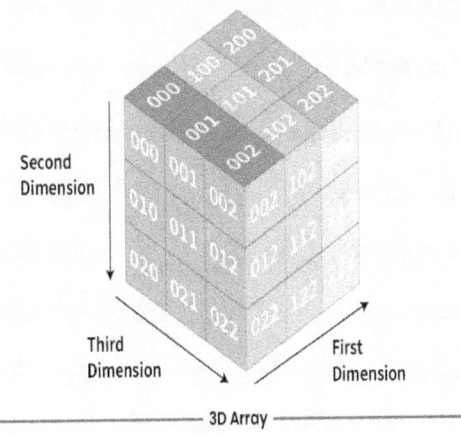

3D Array

Syntax for Declaration
The general syntax for declaring a multi-dimensional array is:
data_type array_name[size1][size2]...[sizeN];
- **data_type**: The type of data the array will hold (e.g., int, float).
- **array_name**: The name of the array.
- **size1, size2, ..., sizeN**: The sizes of each dimension.

Example: Declaration and Initialization of a Three-Dimensional Array
Here's how to declare, initialize, and access elements in a three-dimensional array.

1. Declaration and Initialization

```
#include <stdio.h>

int main() {
   // Declaration and initialization of a 3D integer array (2 x 3 x 4)
   int array[2][3][4] = {
      {
         {1, 2, 3, 4},
         {5, 6, 7, 8},
         {9, 10, 11, 12}
      },
      {
         {13, 14, 15, 16},
         {17, 18, 19, 20},
         {21, 22, 23, 24}
      }
   };

   // Printing the array elements
   printf("3D Array Elements:\n");
   for (int i = 0; i < 2; i++) {
      for (int j = 0; j < 3; j++) {
         for (int k = 0; k < 4; k++) {
            printf("%d ", array[i][j][k]); // Accessing elements
         }
         printf("\n"); // New line for each sub-array
      }
      printf("\n"); // New line for each main array
   }

   return 0;
}
```

Output:
3D Array Elements:
1 2 3 4
5 6 7 8
9 10 11 12

13 14 15 16
17 18 19 20
21 22 23 24

2. Accessing and Modifying Elements
You can access and modify elements in a multi-dimensional array using
#include <stdio.h>

```
int main() {
    // Declaration and initialization of a 3D integer array
    int array[2][2][2] = {
        {
            {1, 2},
            {3, 4}
        },
        {
            {5, 6},
            {7, 8}
        }
    };

    // Accessing and printing a specific element
    printf("Element at (1, 0, 1): %d\n", array[1][0][1]); // Accessing element (5, 6) -> 6

    // Modifying an element
    array[0][1][0] = 99; // Changing the element at (0, 1, 0) from 3 to 99

    // Printing the modified array
    printf("Modified 3D Array Elements:\n");
    for (int i = 0; i < 2; i++) {
        for (int j = 0; j < 2; j++) {
            for (int k = 0; k < 2; k++) {
                printf("%d ", array[i][j][k]); // Accessing each element
            }
            printf("\n");
        }
        printf("\n");
```

```
    }
    return 0;
}
```
Output:
Element at (1, 0, 1): 6
Modified 3D Array Elements:
1 2
99 4

5 6
7 8

Summary
- **Multi-Dimensional Array**: An array with more than two dimensions (e.g., 2D, 3D).
- **Declaration**: The syntax is data_type array_name[size1][size2]...[sizeN];.
- **Initialization**: Elements can be initialized at the time of declaration using nested braces.
- **Accessing Elements**: Use multiple indices, like array[i][j][k], to access specific elements.

Understanding multi-dimensional arrays is important for working with complex data structures in C programming, such as images, matrices, and multi-layered data.

CHAPTER 7: STRINGS

7.1 Strings Introduction
In C, a **string** is a sequence of characters terminated by a null character ('\0'). Unlike many other programming languages, C does not have a built-in string data type. Instead, strings are represented as arrays of characters. A string is a sequence of characters. e.g. "ScholarHat". Many programming languages like Java have a data type known as a string for storing string values. In C, a string is stored as an array of characters. The string is terminated with a null character '\0'. A string is represented using double quotes, ("") or single quotes ("). Whenever an array of characters e.g. c[10] gets created, the compiler implicitly appends '\0' at the end of the string.

Characteristics of Strings in C
1. **Character Array**: A string is essentially an array of characters. For example, the string "Hello" is represented as an array: {'H', 'e', 'l', 'l', 'o', '\0'}.
2. **Null-Terminated**: The string ends with a null character ('\0'), which signifies the end of the string.
3. **Fixed Size**: When declaring a string, the size must be defined if you're using an array. The size should be large enough to accommodate all characters plus the null terminator.

In C programming, a string is a sequence of characters terminated with a null character \0.
For example:
char c[] = "c string";
When the compiler encounters a sequence of characters enclosed in the double quotation marks, it appends a null character \0 at the end by default.

c	s	t	r	i	n	g	\0

7.1.1 Strings Declaration
Syntax
    char variableName[size];
Example
    char str[20];
Here, a string, str gets created that can store 20 characters.

7.1.2 Strings Initialization
There are **many methods** to do this
- **Using char array**

without declaring the size of the array
    char str[] = {'S', 'c', 'h', 'o', 'l', 'a', 'r', 'H', 'a', 't', '\0'};
by declaring the size of the array
    char str[10] = {'S', 'c', 'h', 'o', 'l', 'a', 'r', 'H', 'a', 't', '\0'};
You might have noticed that in this method, we are manually appending '\0' at the end of every string.'\0' is necessary as it indicates the end of the string.
- **Using string literal**

without declaring the size of the array
    char str[]="ScholarHat";
by declaring the size of the array
    char str[10]="ScholarHat";
This is the easiest method. There is no need to manually append a '\0' at the end of the string. When the compiler sees something written in "", it understands it as a string and adds '\0' at the end by default.
- **Pointers to Strings**

You can also declare a string using a pointer to a string literal. This approach is often used for constant strings.
    char *str = "Hello"; // Pointer to a string literal

More Examples
    char c[] = "abcd";
    char c[50] = "abcd";
    char c[] = {'a', 'b', 'c', 'd', '\0'};
    char c[5] = {'a', 'b', 'c', 'd', '\0'};

7.1.3 Reading Strings from Keyboard
In C, you can read strings from the keyboard using standard input functions. The most common functions for reading strings are scanf() and fgets()
- **Using scanf()**

The scanf() function can be used to read a string, but it has some limitations. Specifically, it stops reading input at the first whitespace (space, tab, newline).

```
#include <stdio.h>
int main() {
  char str[100]; // Declare a character array

  printf("Enter a string: ");
  scanf("%99s", str); // Read a string (up to 99 characters to leave space for '\0')

  printf("You entered: %s\n", str); // Print the entered string
```

```
    return 0;
}
```
Output:
Enter a string: Hello World
You entered: Hello
Note: In this example, only "Hello" is captured because scanf() stops reading at the first whitespace.
- **Using fgets()**

The fgets() function is a better option for reading strings, as it can read an entire line, including spaces, until a newline character is encountered or the specified limit is reached.

Example:
```
#include <stdio.h>

int main() {
    char str[100]; // Declare a character array

    printf("Enter a string: ");
    fgets(str, sizeof(str), stdin); // Read a string including spaces

    printf("You entered: %s", str); // Print the entered string

    return 0;
}
```
Output:
Enter a string: Hello World
You entered: Hello World

Differences Between scanf() and fgets()
1. **Whitespace Handling**:
    - scanf() stops reading at the first whitespace.
    - fgets() reads the entire line, including spaces.
2. **Buffer Overflow Protection**:
    - Both methods allow you to limit the number of characters read to prevent buffer overflow. However, with fgets(), you specify the buffer size directly, while scanf() uses a format specifier.
3. **Newline Character**:
    - fgets() retains the newline character in the string, while scanf() does not. You may need to remove it if you don't want it in your output.

Summary
- **scanf()**: Reads a single word (stops at whitespace).
- **fgets()**: Reads a full line (including spaces) and retains the newline character.

- Use strcspn() to remove the newline if necessary.

These methods will help you effectively read strings from the keyboard in C programming.

7.2 String Buit-in Functions

In C programming language, several string functions can be used to manipulate strings. To use them, you must include the **<string.h>** header file in your programThese string functions enable you to perform various operations such as copying, concatenating, comparing, searching, and tokenizing strings in C. Understanding how to use these functions is essential for effective string manipulation in your programs.Here's a table summarizing some commonly used string functions in C, along with their descriptions and example usage.

Function	Description	Example	Output
strlen()	Returns the length of a string (excluding null terminator).	strlen("Hello")	5
strcpy()	Copies one string to another.	char dest[6]; strcpy(dest, "Hi");	dest contains "Hi"
strcat()	Concatenates (appends) one string to another.	char str1[20] = "Hello"; strcat(str1, " World");	str1 contains "Hello World"
strcmp()	Compares two strings. Returns 0 if equal, <0 if first is less, >0 if greater.	strcmp("abc", "abd")	Negative value (e.g., -1)
strchr()	Locates the first occurrence of a character in a string.	strchr("Hello", 'e')	Pointer to "ello"
strstr()	Finds the first occurrence of a substring in a string.	strstr("Hello World", "World")	Pointer to "World"
strncpy()	Copies a specified number of characters from one string to another.	char dest[6]; strncpy(dest, "Hello", 4);	dest contains "Hell"
strncat()	Concatenates a specified number of characters from one string to another.	char str1[20] = "Hello"; strncat(str1, " World", 3);	str1 contains "Hello Wor"

| strtok() | Tokenizes a string into substrings based on delimiters. | strtok("Hello,World", ",") | First call returns "Hello" |
| sprintf() | Formats and stores a string in a buffer (like printf but for strings). | char buffer[50]; sprintf(buffer, "Value: %d", 10); | buffer contains "Value: 10" |

Example Program Demonstrating String Functions

Here's a complete example that showcases several of these string functions:

```
#include <stdio.h>
#include <string.h>

int main() {
    // Example values
    char str1[20] = "Hello";
    char str2[20] = "World";
    char str3[20];
    char *result;

    // Using strlen
    printf("Length of str1: %zu\n", strlen(str1)); // Output: 5

    // Using strcpy
    strcpy(str3, str1);
    printf("str3 after strcpy: %s\n", str3); // Output: Hello

    // Using strcat
    strcat(str1, " ");
    strcat(str1, str2);
    printf("str1 after strcat: %s\n", str1); // Output: Hello World

    // Using strcmp
    int cmpResult = strcmp(str1, str3);
    printf("Comparison result: %d\n", cmpResult); // Output: positive value

    // Using strchr
    result = strchr(str1, 'W');
    if (result) {
        printf("First occurrence of 'W': %s\n", result); // Output: World
    }

    // Using strstr
    result = strstr(str1, "llo");
    if (result) {
```

```c
        printf("Found substring 'llo': %s\n", result); // Output: llo World
    }

    // Using strncpy
    strncpy(str3, str1, 5);
    str3[5] = '\0'; // Null-terminate
    printf("str3 after strncpy: %s\n", str3); // Output: Hello

    // Using strncat
    strncat(str3, " World", 3);
    printf("str3 after strncat: %s\n", str3); // Output: Hello Wor

    // Using strtok
    char tokenString[] = "Hello,World,Example";
    char *token = strtok(tokenString, ",");
    while (token != NULL) {
        printf("Token: %s\n", token); // Output: Hello, World, Example
        token = strtok(NULL, ",");
    }

    // Using sprintf
    char buffer[50];
    sprintf(buffer, "Value: %d", 10);
    printf("%s\n", buffer); // Output: Value: 10

    return 0;
}
```

Here are some example programs demonstrating various string functions in C, along with their expected outputs.

1. Example Using strlen(), strcpy(), and strcat()

```c
#include <stdio.h>
#include <string.h>

int main() {
    char str1[20] = "Hello";
    char str2[20] = "World";
    char result[40];

    // Using strlen
    printf("Length of str1: %zu\n", strlen(str1)); // Output: 5

    // Using strcpy
```

```c
    strcpy(result, str1); // Copy str1 to result
    printf("Copied string: %s\n", result); // Output: Hello

    // Using strcat
    strcat(result, " "); // Add space
    strcat(result, str2); // Concatenate str2 to result
    printf("Concatenated string: %s\n", result); // Output: Hello World

    return 0;
}
```
Output:
Length of str1: 5
Copied string: Hello
Concatenated string: Hello World

2. Example Using strcmp() and strncpy()

```c
#include <stdio.h>
#include <string.h>

int main() {
    char str1[] = "Hello";
    char str2[] = "Hello";
    char str3[10];

    // Using strcmp
    int cmpResult = strcmp(str1, str2);
    printf("Comparison result: %d\n", cmpResult); // Output: 0 (strings are equal)

    // Using strncpy
    strncpy(str3, str1, 3); // Copy first 3 characters
    str3[3] = '\0'; // Null-terminate
    printf("str3 after strncpy: %s\n", str3); // Output: Hel

    return 0;
}
```
Output:
Comparison result: 0
str3 after strncpy: Hel

3. Example Using strchr() and strstr()

```c
#include <stdio.h>
#include <string.h>
```

```c
int main() {
   char str[] = "Hello, World!";

   // Using strchr
   char *ptr = strchr(str, 'W');
   if (ptr) {
      printf("First occurrence of 'W': %s\n", ptr); // Output: World!
   }

   // Using strstr
   char *subPtr = strstr(str, "lo");
   if (subPtr) {
      printf("Found substring 'lo': %s\n", subPtr); // Output: lo, World!
   }

   return 0;
}
```
Output:
First occurrence of 'W': World!
Found substring 'lo': lo, World!

4. Example Using strtok()
```c
#include <stdio.h>
#include <string.h>

int main() {
   char str[] = "Hello,World,Example";
   char *token;

   // Using strtok to split the string by comma
   token = strtok(str, ",");
   while (token != NULL) {
      printf("Token: %s\n", token); // Output each token
      token = strtok(NULL, ",");
   }

   return 0;
}
```
Output:
Token: Hello
Token: World
Token: Example

5. Example Using sprintf()

```
#include <stdio.h>

int main() {
    char buffer[50];
    int value = 10;

    // Using sprintf to format a string
    sprintf(buffer, "The value is: %d", value);
    printf("%s\n", buffer); // Output: The value is: 10

    return 0;
}
```
Output:
The value is: 10

CHAPTER 8: STRUCTURES AND UNIONS

8.1 Structure

In C programming language, a structure is a collection of elements of the different data type. The structure is used to create user-defined data type in the C programming language. As the structure used to create a user-defined data type, the structure is also said to be "user-defined data type in C". In other words, a structure is a collection of non-homogeneous elements. Using structure we can define new data types called user-defined data types that holds multiple values of the different data type. Each element in a structure is called a **member**, and these members can be of different types, including basic data types, arrays, and even other structures.

The formal definition of structure is as follows:

Structure is a colloction of different type of elements under a single name that acts as user defined data type in C.

Generally, structures are used to define a record in the c programming language. Structures allow us to combine elements of a different data type into a group. The elements that are defined in a structure are called members of structure.

Characteristics of Structures in C

1. **Grouping of Different Data Types**:
    - Structures can contain members of various data types, enabling the representation of complex entities.
    - For example, a struct can contain an integer, a float, and a character array all together.
2. **User-Defined Data Type**:
    - Structures allow you to create a new data type that suits your specific needs, making the code more modular and readable.
3. **Accessing Members**:
    - Members of a structure can be accessed using the dot operator (.) when using a structure variable or the arrow operator (->) when using a pointer to a structure.
4. **Memory Allocation**:
    - The size of a structure is the sum of the sizes of its members (with possible padding for alignment). This means structures can take up varying amounts of memory depending on their composition.
5. **Initialization**:
    - Structures can be initialized at the time of declaration using braces {}.

6. **Nested Structures**:
   - Structures can contain other structures as members, allowing for a hierarchical data representation.
7. **Passing Structures**:
   - Structures can be passed to functions by value or by reference, enabling effective data manipulation.

Why Structures

Structures in C are user-defined data types that allow you to group different types of variables under a single name. They provide several advantages:

1. **Grouping Related Data:** Structures enable you to bundle related variables together. This is useful for representing complex data entities that naturally contain multiple attributes. For example, you can group a person's name, age, and height into a single `struct`.

2. **Improved Code Organization:** By using structures, your code becomes more organized and readable. Instead of having multiple unrelated variables, you can encapsulate related data, making it clearer what data belongs together.

3. **Enhanced Data Management:** Structures allow for better management of data, especially when passing multiple related variables to functions. Instead of passing several parameters, you can pass a single structure.

4. **Flexibility:** Structures can contain different data types, which gives you the flexibility to model complex data structures that reflect real-world entities.

5. **Modularity:** Structures promote modular programming. You can define structures once and use them throughout your program, making it easier to maintain and modify your code.

6. **Facilitating Data Structures:** Structures serve as the foundation for more complex data structures, such as linked lists, trees, and graphs. They provide a way to link data elements together.

8.1.2 Creating Structure

How to create a structure

To create structure in c, we use the keyword called "struct". We use the following syntax to create structures in c programming language.

```
struct <structure_name>
{
    data_type member1;
    data_type member2, member3;
    .
    .
};
```

Examples 1:
```
struct Student
{
    char stud_name[30];
```

```
    int roll_number;
    float percentage;
} instance_1,instance_2 instance_n;
```
Examples 2:
```
struct address{
        unsigned int house_number;
        char street_name[50];
        int zip_code;
        char country[50];
};
struct address  instance_1,instance_2 instance_n;
```
Important Points to be Remembered
      Every structure must terminated with semicolon symbol (;).
      "struct" is a keyword, it must be used in lowercase letters only.

Example Program 1
Here's a complete example that combines declaration, variable creation, and initialization.
```
#include <stdio.h>

// Define the structure
struct Person {
   char name[50];
   int age;
   float height;
};

int main() {
   // Declare and initialize structure variables
   struct Person person1 = {"Bob", 25, 5.8};
   struct Person person2; // Declared but not initialized

   // Initialize person2 members individually
   strcpy(person2.name, "Alice");
   person2.age = 30;
   person2.height = 5.6;

   // Print the details
   printf("Person 1: Name: %s, Age: %d, Height: %.1f\n", person1.name, person1.age, person1.height);
   printf("Person 2: Name: %s, Age: %d, Height: %.1f\n", person2.name, person2.age, person2.height);
```

    return 0;
}
Output:
Person 1: Name: Bob, Age: 25, Height: 5.8
Person 2: Name: Alice, Age: 30, Height: 5.6

Summary of Structure Declaration Steps
1. **Define the Structure**: Use struct followed by the structure name and its members.
2. **Declare Structure Variables**: Create variables of the defined structure type.
3. **Initialize Structure Variables**: You can initialize them at the time of declaration or set their members individually afterward.

This way, you can create complex data types that suit your specific needs in C programming.

Example Program 2

```
struct Student
{
   char stud_name[30];
   int roll_number;
   float percentage;
} stud_1 ;          // while defining structure

void main(){
   struct Student stud_2;  // using struct keyword

   printf("Enter details of stud_1 : \n");
   printf("Name : ");
   scanf("%s", stud_1.stud_name);
   printf("Roll Number : ");
   scanf("%d", &stud_1.roll_number);
   printf("Percentage : ");
   scanf("%f", &stud_1.percentage);

   printf("***** Student 1 Details *****\n);
   printf("Name of the Student : %s\n", stud_1.stud_name);
   printf("Roll Number of the Student : %i\n", stud_1.roll_number);
   printf("Percentage of the Student : %f\n", stud_1.percentage);
}
```

In the above example program, the stucture variable "**stud_1** is created while defining the structure and the variable "**stud_2** is careted using struct keyword. Whenever we access the members of a structure we use the dot (.) operator.

8.1.3 Memory allocation of Structure

When the structures are used in the c programming language, the memory does not allocate on defining a structure. The memory is allocated when we create the variable of a particular structure. As long as the variable of a structure is created no memory is allocated. The size of memory allocated is equal to the sum of memory required by individual members of that structure. In the above example program, the variables stud_1 and stud_2 are allocated with 36 bytes of memory each.

```
struct Student{
    char stud_name[30];  ──── 30 bytes
    int roll_number;     ──── 02 bytes
    float percentage;    ──── 04 bytes
};                          sum = 36 bytes
```

Here the variable of Student structure is allocated with 36 bytes of memory

Important Points to be Remembered

All the members of a structure can be used simultaneously.
Until variable of a structure is created no memory is allocated.
The memory required by a structure variable is sum of the memory required by individual members of that structure

Example 2: Memory Occupied by a Structure
Now, let's create a structure with the same elements and check how much space it occupies in the memory.

```
#include <stdio.h>
#include <string.h>

struct Data{
  int i;
  float f;
  char str[20];
};

int main(){
  struct Data data;
  printf("Memory occupied by Struct Data: %d \n", sizeof(data));
  return 0;
}
```

Output

This stucture will occupy 28 bytes (4 + 4 + 20). Run the code and check its output −
Memory occupied by Struct Data: 28

8.2 Union
In C, a union is a special data structure that allows you to store different data types in the same memory location. This means that a union can hold only one of its members at any given time, making it memory efficient when you need to use different types but not at the same time.

Characteristics of Unions:
1. **Single Storage Location**:
   - All members of a union share the same memory location. The size of the union is determined by the size of its largest member.
2. **Memory Efficiency**:
   - Since only one member can be used at a time, unions can be more memory-efficient compared to structures, which allocate memory for all members.
3. **Accessing Members**:
   - You can access the members using the dot (.) operator for union variables. However, since only one member holds a valid value at any time, you must be careful to use the correct member.
4. **Initialization**:
   - You can initialize a union, but only the first member can be initialized directly. The other members will contain indeterminate values unless explicitly set later.
5. **Type Safety**:
   - Unions do not provide type safety. It's up to the programmer to ensure that the correct member is accessed, as accessing a member that hasn't been assigned a value can lead to undefined behavior.
6. **Use Cases**:
   - Unions are commonly used in scenarios where you need to handle different types of data but know that only one will be used at a time. They are often seen in embedded systems, protocol data structures, and situations where memory conservation is crucial.

Why Unions
Unions are useful in C for several reasons:
1. Memory Efficiency
- Unions allow multiple data types to share the same memory space. This can save memory when you only need to use one type at a time, making

them ideal for applications where memory usage is a concern, such as embedded systems.

2. Flexibility
- Unions provide a way to handle different data types in a single variable. This is useful in scenarios like protocol handling, where the type of data can vary (e.g., integers, floats, strings).

3. Data Type Variability
- They enable functions or structures to work with various data types without needing to create separate variables for each type. This can simplify code and improve maintainability.

4. Simplified Structures
- Unions can be combined with structures to create complex data types that can store various forms of related data. For example, you might have a structure representing a network packet that can contain either an IP address or a MAC address, depending on the context.

5. Performance
- In some cases, using a union can lead to performance improvements. Since unions only allocate enough memory for the largest member, they can reduce the overhead associated with managing multiple variables.

Use Cases
- **Networking Protocols**: Handling different types of data packets in a single structure.
- **Embedded Systems**: Managing sensor data where different types of readings may be processed.
- **Type Conversions**: Converting data types without using additional memory.

Example Scenario
Consider a graphics program that can handle different shapes (like circles, rectangles, etc.). You could use a union to store the dimensions for each shape type, which reduces the memory footprint by ensuring that only the relevant data is stored for any given shape at a time.

In summary, unions provide a way to efficiently manage memory and handle different data types, making them a valuable tool in C programming.

8.2.1 Union Declaration
Syntax of Union in C

Unions in C are user-defined data types that allow different data members to share the same memory space. The syntax to declare a union is with the union keyword, similar to the way struct is used for structures.

```
union unionName {
    member definition;
    member definition;
```

```
    ...
} [unionVar1, unionVar2, ...];
```
Example
```
union circle
{
   char name[30];
   int radius;
} circle1, circle2;
```
The declaration above includes a union named "circle" with two members, name and radius. At the same time, two union variables circle1 and circle2 are created.

Different Ways to Define a Union Variable
Union variables can be defined in multiple ways:
- **Defining Union Variable with Declaration**

When you declare a union, you can simultaneously define union variables:
```
union student {
   char name[50];
   int roll_no;
} stud1, stud2;
```
In the example above, stud1 and stud2 are union variables declared alongside the student union.

- **Defining Union Variable after Declaration**

Alternatively, union variables can be defined separately after the union's declaration:
```
union student {
   char name[50];
   int roll_no;
};
union student stud1, stud2;
```
Here, the union variables stud1 and stud2 are defined after the student union declaration.

Important Points to be Remembered
Every union must terminated with semicolon symbol (;).
"union" is a keyword, it must be used in lowercase letters only.

8.2.2 Accessing the Union Members
To access any member of a union, we use the member access operator (.). The member access operator is coded as a period between the union variable name and the union member that we wish to access. You would use the keyword union to define variables of union type.

Syntax
Here is the syntax to access the members of a union in C language –

union_name.member_name;

8.2.3 Initialization of Union Members
You can initialize the members of the union by assigning the value to them using the assignment (=) operator.
Syntax
Here is the syntax to initialize members of union –
　　union_variable.member_name = value;
Example
The following code statement shows to initialization of the member "i" of union "data" –
data.i = 10;
Example of Union
```
#include <stdio.h>
#include <string.h>

union Data{
  int i;
  float f;
  char str[20];
};

int main(){
  union Data data;

  data.i = 10;
  data.f = 220.5;
  strcpy(data.str, "C Programming");

  printf("data.i: %d \n", data.i);
  printf("data.f: %f \n", data.f);
  printf("data.str: %s \n", data.str);
  return 0;
}
```
Output:
data.i: 1917853763
data.f: 4122360580327794860452759994368.000000
data.str: C Programming

Example of Union
```c
#include <stdio.h>

// Define a union named MyUnion
union MyUnion {
    int intValue;
    float floatValue;
    char stringValue[20];
};

int main() {
    // Declare an instance of the union
    union MyUnion data;

    // Assign values to different members of the union
    data.intValue = 42;
    printf("Integer Value: %d\n", data.intValue);

    data.floatValue = 3.14;
    printf("Float Value: %.2f\n", data.floatValue);

    // Assign a string to the union
    strcpy(data.stringValue, "Hello, Union!");
    printf("String Value: %s\n", data.stringValue);

    return 0;
}
```
Output
Integer Value: 42
Float Value: 3.14
String Value: Hello, Union!

8.2.4 Size and memory allocation of Union
Size of Union
The size of a union in C is determined by the size of its largest member. The idea is that all members of a union share the same memory space, so the union's size needs to be large enough to accommodate its largest member.

The size of a union is the size of its largest member. For example, if a union contains two members of **char** and **int** types. In that case, the size of the union will be the size of **int** because **int** is the largest member.

You can use the sizeof() operator to get the size of a union.

Memory allocation of Union

When the unions are used in the c programming language, the memory does not allocate on defining union. The memory is allocated when we create the variable of a particular union. As long as the variable of a union is created no memory is allocated. The size of memory allocated is equal to the maximum memory required by an individual member among all members of that union. In the above example program, the variables stud_1 and stud_2 are allocated with 30 bytes of memory each.

```
union Student{
    char stud_name[30];      ──── 30 bytes
    int roll_number;         ──── 02 bytes
    float percentage;        ──── 04 bytes
};                           max = 30 bytes
```

Example 1:
In the following example, we are printing the size of a union –
#include <stdio.h>

// Define a union
union Data {
  int a;
  float b;
  char c[20];
};

int main() {
  union Data data;

  // Printing the size of the each member of union
  printf("Size of a: %lu bytes\n", sizeof(data.a));
  printf("Size of b: %lu bytes\n", sizeof(data.b));
  printf("Size of c: %lu bytes\n", sizeof(data.c));

  // Printing the size of the union
  printf("Size of union: %lu bytes\n", sizeof(data));

  return 0;
}
Output
When you compile and execute the code, it will produce the following output –
Size of a: 4 bytes
Size of b: 4 bytes
Size of c: 20 bytes
Size of union: 20 bytes

Example 2: Basic Union Usage

```c
#include <stdio.h>

union Data {
    int intValue;
    float floatValue;
    char charValue;
};

int main() {
    union Data data;

    data.intValue = 10;
    printf("Int Value: %d\n", data.intValue);

    data.floatValue = 5.5;
    printf("Float Value: %f\n", data.floatValue); // intValue is now lost

    data.charValue = 'A';
    printf("Char Value: %c\n", data.charValue); // previous values are lost

    return 0;
}
```

Expected Output:
kotlin
Copy code
Int Value: 10
Float Value: 5.500000
Char Value: A

Example 2: Using Unions in a Struct

```c
#include <stdio.h>

struct Item {
    int type; // 0 for int, 1 for float, 2 for char
    union Data {
        int intValue;
        float floatValue;
        char charValue;
```

```c
    } data;
};

int main() {
    struct Item item;

    // Set item as an integer
    item.type = 0;
    item.data.intValue = 42;
    printf("Item Type: %d, Value: %d\n", item.type, item.data.intValue);

    // Set item as a float
    item.type = 1;
    item.data.floatValue = 3.14;
    printf("Item Type: %d, Value: %f\n", item.type, item.data.floatValue);

    // Set item as a char
    item.type = 2;
    item.data.charValue = 'Z';
    printf("Item Type: %d, Value: %c\n", item.type, item.data.charValue);

    return 0;
}
```
Expected Output:
Item Type: 0, Value: 42
Item Type: 1, Value: 3.140000
Item Type: 2, Value: Z

Example 3: Handling Multiple Data Types with Unions
```c
#include <stdio.h>
#include <string.h>

union Value {
    int intValue;
    float floatValue;
    char strValue[20];
};

int main() {
    union Value val;

    // Store an integer
    val.intValue = 100;
    printf("Integer: %d\n", val.intValue);
```

```c
    // Store a float
    val.floatValue = 98.6;
    printf("Float: %f\n", val.floatValue); // integer value is now lost

    // Store a string
    strcpy(val.strValue, "Hello");
    printf("String: %s\n", val.strValue); // previous values are now lost

    return 0;
}
```
Expected Output:
Integer: 100
Float: 98.600000
String: Hello

Example 4: Union for Network Data Types
```c
#include <stdio.h>
#include <stdint.h>

union NetworkData {
    uint32_t ip;        // IPv4
    uint16_t port;      // Port number
    uint8_t mac[6];     // MAC address
};

int main() {
    union NetworkData data;

    // Using the union for an IP address
    data.ip = 0xC0A80001; // 192.168.0.1
    printf("IP Address: %u\n", data.ip);

    // Using the union for a port number
    data.port = 8080;
    printf("Port: %u\n", data.port); // ip value is now lost

    // Using the union for a MAC address
    data.mac[0] = 0x00;
    data.mac[1] = 0x1A;
    data.mac[2] = 0x2B;
    data.mac[3] = 0x3C;
    data.mac[4] = 0x4D;
    data.mac[5] = 0x5E;
```

```
    printf("MAC Address: %02X:%02X:%02X:%02X:%02X:%02X\n",
        data.mac[0], data.mac[1], data.mac[2],
        data.mac[3], data.mac[4], data.mac[5]);

    return 0;
}
```
Expected Output:
IP Address: 192168001
Port: 8080
MAC Address: 00:1A:2B:3C:4D:5E

Summary

These programs illustrate how to use unions in different scenarios, with outputs showing how the data is stored and accessed. Keep in mind that only one member of the union can hold a meaningful value at a time.

```
#include <stdio.h>
union unionJob
{
  //defining a union
  char name[32];
  float salary;
  int workerNo;
} uJob;

struct structJob
{
  char name[32];
  float salary;
  int workerNo;
} sJob;

int main()
{
  printf("size of union = %d bytes", sizeof(uJob));
  printf("\nsize of structure = %d bytes", sizeof(sJob));
  return 0;
}
size of union = 32
size of structure = 40
```

Why this difference in the size of union and structure variables?

Here, the size of sJob is 40 bytes because
- the size of name[32] is 32 bytes
- the size of salary is 4 bytes

- the size of workerNo is 4 bytes

However, the size of uJob is 32 bytes. It's because the size of a union variable will always be the size of its largest element. In the above example, the size of its largest element, (name[32]), is 32 bytes.

With a union, all members share **the same memory**.

8.2.5 Difference between Structure and Union

Differences between structure and union are given below table are:

Feature	C Union	C Structure
Memory Allocation	Shares memory space among all members.	Each member has its memory space.
Memory Usage	Shares memory, using the largest member's size.	Requires memory for each member simultaneously.
Accessing Members	Members share the same memory space.	Members are accessed individually.
Size Calculation	Size is the size of the largest member.	Size is the sum of sizes of its members.
Memory Wastage	No wastage as it uses the size of the largest member.	Can lead to memory wastage for small types.
Initialization	All members share the same memory, so initializing one affects others.	Each member can be initialized separately.
Usage	Suitable when only one of the data types is used at a time to save memory.	Suitable when different data types are needed.
Example	c union Number { int x; float y; };	c struct Point { int x; int y; };

8.3 Typedef and Enumerations

In C programming language, an enumeration is used to create user-defined datatypes. Using enumeration, integral constants are assigned with names and we use these names in the program. Using names in programming makes it more readable and easy to maintain.

Enumeration is the process of creating user defined datatype by assigning names to integral constants

We use the keyword **enum** to create enumerated datatype. The general syntax of enum is as follows...

     enum {name1, name2, name3, ... }

In the above syntax, integral constant '0' is assigned to name1, integral constant '1' is assigned to name2 and so on. We can also assign our own integral constants as follows...

enum {name1 = 10, name2 = 30, name3 = 15, ... }

In the above syntax, integral constant '10' is assigned to name1, integral constant '30' is assigned to name2 and so on.

In C, an enumeration (enum) is a user-defined data type that consists of integral constants, making code more readable and maintainable. An enum allows you to define a set of named integer constants that can be used to represent related values.

Characteristics of Enumerations in C:

1. **Definition**: An enumeration is defined using the enum keyword followed by the name of the enumeration and a list of enumerators (named constants) within curly braces. For example,

```
enum Color {
  RED,
  GREEN,
  BLUE
};
```

2. **Underlying Type**: By default, the underlying type of an enum is int. The first enumerator is assigned the value 0, and each subsequent enumerator is assigned the value of the previous enumerator plus one. You can also specify custom values.

```
enum Color {
  RED = 1,
  GREEN = 2,
  BLUE = 4
};
```

3. **Type Safety**: Enums provide a level of type safety compared to using plain integers. This helps prevent errors, as you can't mix enum values with integers without explicit casting.

4. **Scoped Names**: Enumerators within an enum have a global scope (if defined outside any function), which means they can be accessed anywhere in the file after the enum declaration. However, if you define an enum within a function, its enumerators will only be visible within that function.

5. **Readability**: Using enums makes code more understandable. Instead of using arbitrary integers, you can use meaningful names.

```
enum Status {
  SUCCESS,
  FAILURE,
  PENDING
};
```

enum Status taskStatus = SUCCESS;

6. **Implicit Conversion**: Enums can be implicitly converted to integers. You can use them in arithmetic operations or comparisons without needing explicit conversion.
7. **Flexible Enumeration Values**: You can explicitly assign values to enumerators, allowing you to create non-sequential sets of values.
8. **Bit Fields**: Enums can be used in bitwise operations if their values are powers of two, allowing you to combine multiple flags.

Example Usage:

```c
#include <stdio.h>

enum Day {
    SUNDAY,
    MONDAY,
    TUESDAY,
    WEDNESDAY,
    THURSDAY,
    FRIDAY,
    SATURDAY
};

int main() {
    enum Day today = WEDNESDAY;

    if (today == WEDNESDAY) {
        printf("It's midweek!\n");
    }

    return 0;
}
```

Enums in C are a powerful tool for defining sets of related constants, improving code readability, and reducing the chance of errors by providing type safety. They help organize code by replacing magic numbers with meaningful names, making the program easier to understand and maintain.

CHAPTER 9: POINTERS

9.1 Pointer Introduction
Address of a variable:
Address of a variable refers to the memory location where that variable is stored. Each variable in a program is allocated a specific location in memory, and this location can be identified by its address.

For example, If you have a variable var in your program, &var will give you its address in the memory.

We have used address numerous times while using the scanf() function.
scanf("%d", &var);

Here, the value entered by the user is stored in the address of var variable. Let's take a working example.

```
#include <stdio.h>
int main()
{
  int var = 5;
  printf("var: %d\n", var);

  // Notice the use of & before var
  printf("address of var: %p", &var);
  return 0;
}
```

Output:
var: 5
address of var: 2686778

Pointers
In the c programming language, we use normal variables to store user data values. When we declare a variable, the compiler allocates required memory with the specified name. In the c programming language, every variable has a name, datatype, value, storage class, and address. We use a special type of variable called a pointer to store the address of another variable with the same datatype. A pointer is defined as follows....

Pointer is a special type of variable used to store the memory location address of a variable.

Pointers are powerful tools that enable direct memory management and manipulation, which can lead to more efficient programs.

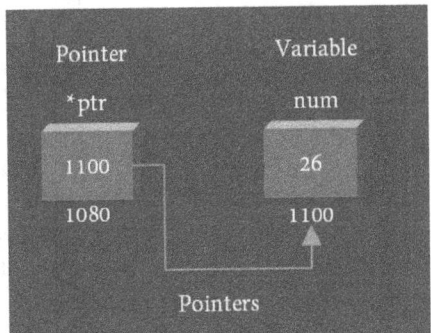

In the c programming language, we can create pointer variables of any datatype. Every pointer stores the address the variable with same datatype only. That means integer pointer is used store the address of integer variable only.

Accessing the Address of Variables
In c programming language, we use the **reference operator "&"** to access the address of variable. For example, to access the address of a variable **"marks"** we use **"&marks"**. We use the following printf statement to display memory location address of variable **"marks"**...
Example Code
    printf("Address : %u", &marks) ;
In the above example statement **%u** is used to display address of **marks** variable. Address of any memory location is unsigned integer value.

Declaring Pointers (Creating Pointers)
In c programming language, declaration of pointer variable is similar to the creation of normal variable but the name is prefixed with * symbol. We use the following syntax to declare a pointer variable...
    datatype *pointerName ;
Example Code
    int *ptr ;
In the above example declaration, the variable **"ptr"** is a pointer variable that can be used to store any integer variable address.
Pointers declarations are:
    int* p;
Here, we have declared a pointer p of int type.
You can also declare pointers in these ways.
    int *p1;
    int * p2;
Let's take another example of declaring pointers.
    int* p1, p2;
Here, we have declared a pointer p1 and a normal variable p2.

Assigning Address to Pointer
Pointer variables are used to store the address of other variables. We can use this address to access the value of the variable through its pointer. We use the symbol **"*"** infront of pointer variable name to access the value of variable to which the pointer is pointing. We use the following general syntax...
> ***pointerVariableName**

To assign address to a pointer variable we use assignment operator with the following syntax...
> **pointerVariableName = & variableName ;**

For example, consider the following variables declaration...
Example Program
> int a, *ptr ;

In the above declaration, variable **"a"** is a normal integer variable and variable **"ptr"** is an integer pointer variable. If we want to assign the address of variable **"a"** to pointer variable **"ptr"** we use the following statement...
Example Code
> ptr = &a ;

In the above statement, the address of variable **"a"** is assigned to pointer variable **"prt"**. Here we say that pointer variable **ptr** is pointing to variable **a**. Let's take an example.
int* pc, c;
c = 5;
pc = &c;
Here, 5 is assigned to the c variable. And, the address of c is assigned to the pc pointer.
Example Code
```
#include<stdio.h>
#include<conio.h>

void main()
{
  int a = 10, *ptr ;
  clrscr();
  ptr = &a ;

  printf("Address of variable a = %u\n", ptr) ;
  printf("Value of variable a = %d\n", *ptr) ;
  printf("Address of variable ptr = %u\n", &ptr) ;
```

}
Output:
Address of variable a=64679
Value of variable a=10
Address of variable ptr=76435
In the above example program, variable **a** is a normal variable and variable **ptr** is a pointer variable. Address of variable **a** is stored in pointer variable **ptr**. Here **ptr** is used to access the address of variable **a** and ***ptr** is used to access the value of variable **a**.

```c
#include <stdio.h>
int main()
{
  int* pc, c;

  c = 22;
  printf("Address of c: %p\n", &c);
  printf("Value of c: %d\n\n", c);  // 22

  pc = &c;
  printf("Address of pointer pc: %p\n", pc);
  printf("Content of pointer pc: %d\n\n", *pc);  // 22

  c = 11;
  printf("Address of pointer pc: %p\n", pc);
  printf("Content of pointer pc: %d\n\n", *pc);  // 11

  *pc = 2;
  printf("Address of c: %p\n", &c);
  printf("Value of c: %d\n\n", c);  // 2
  return 0;
}
```

Output
Address of c: 2686784
Value of c: 22

Address of pointer pc: 2686784
Content of pointer pc: 22

Address of pointer pc: 2686784
Content of pointer pc: 11

Address of c: 2686784
Value of c: 2

Explanation of the program
1. int* pc, c;

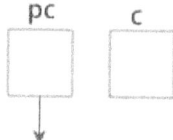

   Here, a pointer pc and a normal variable c, both of type int, is created. Since pc and c are not initialized at initially, pointer pc points to either no address or a random address. And, variable c has an address but contains random garbage value.

2. c = 22;

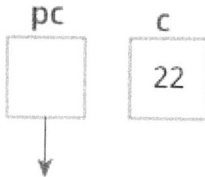

   This assigns 22 to the variable c. That is, 22 is stored in the memory location of variable c.

3. pc = &c;

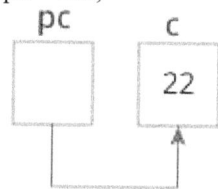

   This assigns the address of variable c to the pointer pc.

4. c = 11;

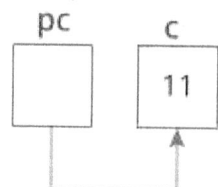

   This assigns 11 to variable c.

5. *pc = 2;

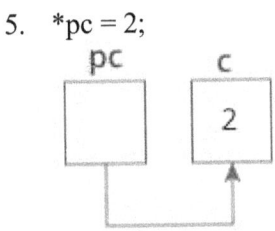

This change the value at the memory location pointed by the pointer pc to 2.

Memory Allocation of Pointer Variables
Every pointer variable is used to store the address of another variable. In computer memory address of any memory location is an **unsigned integer** value. In c programming language, unsigned integer requires **2 bytes** of memory. So, irrespective of pointer datatype every pointer variable is allocated with 2 bytes of memory.

9.1.1 Pointers Arithmetic Operations in C
Pointer variables are used to store the address of variables. Address of any variable is an unsigned integer value i.e., it is a numerical value. So we can perform arithmetic operations on pointer values. But when we perform arithmetic operations on pointer variable, the result depends on the amount of memory required by the variable to which the pointer is pointing.

In the c programming language, we can perform the following arithmetic operations on pointers...
 1. Addition
 2. Subtraction
 3. Increment
 4. Decrement
 5. Comparison

Addition Operation on Pointer
In the c programming language, the addition operation on pointer variables is calculated using the following formula...

    AddressAtPointer + (NumberToBeAdd * BytesOfMemoryRequiredByDatatype)

Example Program
```
void main()
{
  int a, *intPtr ;
  float b, *floatPtr ;
```

```c
  double c, *doublePtr ;
  clrscr() ;
  intPtr = &a ;  // Asume address of a is 1000
  floatPtr = &b ;  // Asume address of b is 2000
  doublePtr = &c ;  // Asume address of c is 3000

  intPtr = intPtr + 3 ;  // intPtr = 1000 + ( 3 * 2 )
  floatPtr = floatPtr + 2 ;  // floatPtr = 2000 + ( 2 * 4 )
  doublePtr = doublePtr + 5 ;  // doublePtr = 3000 + ( 5 * 6 )

  printf("intPtr value : %u\n", intPtr) ;
  printf("floatPtr value : %u\n", floatPtr) ;
  printf("doublePtr value : %u", doublePtr) ;

  getch() ;
}
```

```
intPtr value : 6356748
floatPtr value : 6356740
doublePtr value : 6356760
```

Subtraction Operation on Pointer

In the c programming language, the subtraction operation on pointer variables is calculated using the following formula...

　　　AddressAtPointer - (NumberToBeAdd *
　　　BytesOfMemoryRequiredByDatatype)

Example Program

```c
void main()
{
  int a, *intPtr ;
  float b, *floatPtr ;
  double c, *doublePtr ;
  clrscr() ;
  intPtr = &a ;  // Asume address of a is 1000
  floatPtr = &b ;  // Asume address of b is 2000
  doublePtr = &c ;  // Asume address of c is 3000

  intPtr = intPtr - 3 ;  // intPtr = 1000 - ( 3 * 2 )
  floatPtr = floatPtr - 2 ;  // floatPtr = 2000 - ( 2 * 4 )
  doublePtr = doublePtr - 5 ;  // doublePtr = 3000 - ( 5 * 6 )

  printf("intPtr value : %u\n", intPtr) ;
  printf("floatPtr value : %u\n", floatPtr) ;
  printf("doublePtr value : %u", doublePtr) ;

  getch() ;
```

}
Output:
```
intPtr value : 6356724
floatPtr value : 6356724
doublePtr value : 6356680
```
Increment & Decrement Operation on Pointer
The increment operation on pointer variable is calculated as follows...
        AddressAtPointer + NumberOfBytesRequiresByDatatype
Example Program
```c
void main()
{
  int a, *intPtr ;
  float b, *floatPtr ;
  double c, *doublePtr ;
  clrscr() ;
  intPtr = &a ;   // Asume address of a is 1000
  floatPtr = &b ;  // Asume address of b is 2000
  doublePtr = &c ;  // Asume address of c is 3000

  intPtr++ ;    // intPtr = 1000 + 2
  floatPtr++ ;   // floatPtr = 2000 + 4
  doublePtr++ ;  // doublePtr = 3000 + 6

  printf("intPtr value : %u\n", intPtr) ;
  printf("floatPtr value : %u\n", floatPtr) ;
  printf("doublePtr value : %u", doublePtr) ;

  getch() ;
}
```
Output:
```
intPtr value : 6356740
floatPtr value : 6356736
doublePtr value : 6356728
```
The decrement operation on pointer variable is calculated as follows...
        AddressAtPointer - NumberOfBytesRequiresByDatatype
Example Program
```c
void main()
{
  int a, *intPtr ;
  float b, *floatPtr ;
  double c, *doublePtr ;
  clrscr() ;
  intPtr = &a ;   // Asume address of a is 1000
  floatPtr = &b ;  // Asume address of b is 2000
  doublePtr = &c ;  // Asume address of c is 3000
```

```
   intPtr-- ;   // intPtr = 1000 - 2
   floatPtr-- ;   // floatPtr = 2000 - 4
   doublePtr-- ;   // doublePtr = 3000 - 6

   printf("intPtr value : %u\n", intPtr) ;
   printf("floatPtr value : %u\n", floatPtr) ;
   printf("doublePtr value : %u", doublePtr) ;

   getch() ;
}
```
Output:

```
intPtr value : 6356732
floatPtr value : 6356728
doublePtr value : 6356712
```

Comparison of Pointers
The comparison operation is perform between the pointers of same datatype only. In c programming language, we can use all comparison operators (relational operators) with pointers.

9.1.2 Pointers to Pointers in C
In the c programming language, we have pointers to store the address of variables of any datatype. A pointer variable can store the address of a normal variable. C programming language also provides a pointer variable to store the address of another pointer variable. This type of pointer variable is called a pointer to pointer variable. Sometimes we also call it a double pointer. We use the following syntax for creating pointer to pointer...
  datatype **pointerName ;
Example
  int **ptr ;
Here, **ptr** is an integer pointer variable that stores the address of another integer pointer variable but does not stores the normal integer variable address.

Most Important Points To Be Remembered
1. To store the address of normal variable we use single pointer variable
2. To store the address of single pointer variable we use double pointer variable
3. To store the address of double pointer variable we use triple pointer variable
4. Similarly the same for remaining pointer variables also...

Example Program
#include<stdio.h>
#include<conio.h>

```
int main()
{
  int a ;
  int *ptr1 ;
  int **ptr2 ;
  int ***ptr3 ;

  ptr1 = &a ;
  ptr2 = &ptr1 ;
  ptr3 = &ptr2 ;

  printf("\nAddress of normal variable 'a' = %u\n", ptr1) ;
  printf("Address of pointer variable '*ptr1' = %u\n", ptr2) ;
  printf("Address of pointer-to-pointer '**ptr2' = %u\n", ptr3) ;
  return 0;
}
```
Output:
```
Address of normal variable 'a' = 6356744
Address of pointer variable '*ptr1' = 6356740
Address of pointer-to-pointer '**ptr2' = 6356736
```

9.1.3 Pointers to Arrays in C
In the c programming language, when we declare an array the compiler allocate the required amount of memory and also creates a constant pointer with array name and stores the base address of that pointer in it. The address of the first element of an array is called as **base address** of that array. The array name itself acts as a pointer to the first element of that array. Consider the following example of array declaration...

Example Code
        int marks[6] ;
For the above declaration, the compiler allocates 12 bytes of memory and the address of first memory location (i.e., marks[0]) is stored in a constant pointer called **marks**. That means in the above example, **marks** is a pointer to **marks[0]**.

Example Program
```
#include<stdio.h>
#include<conio.h>

int main()
{
  int marks[6] = {89, 45, 58, 72, 90, 93} ;
  int *ptr ;

  clrscr() ;
```

```
ptr = marks ;
printf("Base Address of 'marks' array = %u\n", ptr) ;
return 0;
}
```
Output:

Base Address of 'marks' array = 6356724

Most Important Points To Be Remembered
1. An array name is a **constant pointer**.
2. We can use the array name to access the address and value of all the elements of that array.
3. Since array name is a constant pointer we can't modify its value.

Consider the following example statements...

Example Code
```
ptr = marks + 2 ;
```
Here, the pointer variable **"ptr"** is assigned with address of **"marks[2]"** element.

Example Code
```
printf("Address of 'marks[4]' = %u", marks+4) ;
```
The above printf statement displays the address of element **"marks[4]"**.

Example Code
```
printf("Value of 'marks[0]' = %d", *marks) ;
printf("Value of 'marks[3]' = %d", *(marks+3)) ;
```
In the above two statements, first printf statement prints the value **89** (i.e., value of marks[0]) and the second printf statement prints the value **72** (i.e., value of marks[3]).

Example Code
```
marks++ ;
```
The above statement generates **compilation error** because the array name acts as a constant pointer. So we can't change its value.

In the above example program, the array name **marks** can be used as follows...

marks is same as **&marks[0]**
marks + 1 is same as **&marks[1]**
marks + 2 is same as **&marks[2]**
marks + 3 is same as **&marks[3]**
marks + 4 is same as **&marks[4]**
marks + 5 is same as **&marks[5]**
*****marks** is same as **marks[0]**
*****(marks + 1)** is same as **marks[1]**
*****(marks + 2)** is same as **marks[2]**
*****(marks + 3)** is same as **marks[3]**
*****(marks + 4)** is same as **marks[4]**
*****(marks + 5)** is same as **marks[5]**

Pointers to Multi-Dimensional Array
In case of multi dimensional array also the array name acts as a constant pointer to the base address of that array. For example, we declare an array as follows...
Example Code
        int marks[3][3] ;
In the above example declaration, the array name **marks** acts as constant pointer to the base address (**address of marks[0][0]**) of that array.
In the above example of two dimensional array, the element **marks[1][2]** is accessed as *(*(marks + 1) + 2).

9.1.4 Pointers for Functions in C
In the c programming language, there are two ways to pass parameters to functions. They are as follows...
  1. Call by Value
  2. Call By Reference

We use pointer variables as formal parameters in **call by reference** parameter passing method.
In case of **call by reference** parameter passing method, the address of actual parameters is passed as arguments from the calling function to the called function. To recieve this address, we use pointer variables as formal parameters.
In C, there are two primary methods of passing arguments to functions: **call by value** and **call by reference**. Each method has distinct characteristics and use cases.

Call by Value
In **call by value**, a copy of the actual argument's value is passed to the function. Changes made to the parameter inside the function do not affect the original variable.

Characteristics:
  1. **Copies the Value**: Only the value of the argument is copied, not the actual variable.
  2. **No Side Effects**: Modifications to the parameter within the function do not affect the original variable.
  3. **Safer**: It avoids unintentional modifications to the original data.

Example Program:
```
#include <stdio.h>

void modifyValue(int x) {
    x = 100; // Change will not affect the original variable
}

int main() {
    int num = 42;
    printf("Before function call: %d\n", num); // Output: 42
```

```
    modifyValue(num);
    printf("After function call: %d\n", num);  // Output: 42 (unchanged)
    return 0;
}
```
Call by Reference
In **call by reference**, instead of passing a copy of the variable, a reference (or address) to the original variable is passed. Changes made to the parameter inside the function affect the original variable.

Characteristics:
1. **Uses Pointers**: The function receives the address of the variable, allowing direct modification.
2. **Side Effects**: Modifications to the parameter within the function will change the original variable.
3. **More Efficient for Large Data**: Passing large structures or arrays by reference avoids copying large amounts of data.

Example Program:
```c
#include <stdio.h>

void modifyValue(int *x) {
    *x = 100; // Change will affect the original variable
}

int main() {
    int num = 42;
    printf("Before function call: %d\n", num); // Output: 42
    modifyValue(&num); // Pass the address of num
    printf("After function call: %d\n", num); // Output: 100 (changed)
    return 0;
}
```

Summary
- **Call by Value**:
    - Passes a copy of the variable's value.
    - Original variable remains unchanged.
    - Safer and simpler for basic data types.
- **Call by Reference**:
    - Passes the address of the variable.
    - Original variable can be modified.
    - More efficient for large data structures.

Both methods have their own advantages and use cases, and understanding them is essential for effective C programming.

Consider the following program for swapping two variable values...
Example - Swapping of two variable values using Call by Reference
#include<stdio.h>
#include<conio.h>

void swap(int *, int *) ;

void main()
{
　int a = 10, b = 20 ;

　clrscr() ;

　printf("Before swap : a = %d and b = %d\n", a, b) ;

　swap(&a, &b) ;

　printf("After swap : a = %d and b = %d\n", a, b) ;

　getch() ;
}
void swap(int *x, int *y)
{
　int temp ;
　temp = *x ;
　*x = *y ;
　*y = temp ;
}
Output:
```
Before swap : a = 10 and b = 20
After swap  : a = 20 and b = 10
```
In the above example program, we are passing the addresses of variables **a** and **b** and these are recieved by the pointer variables **x** and **y**. In the called function **swap** we use the pointer variables **x** and **y** to swap the values of variables **a** and **b**.

9.2 Dynamic Memory Allocation
Understanding Dynamic Memory Allocation
Dynamic memory allocation in C refers to the process of allocating memory at runtime, allowing programs to request and release memory as needed. This is particularly useful when the size of data structures cannot be determined at compile time.

As you know, an array is a collection of a fixed number of values. Once the size of an array is declared, you cannot change it.
Sometimes the size of the array you declared may be insufficient. To solve this issue, you can allocate memory manually during run-time. This is known as dynamic memory allocation in C programming.
To allocate memory dynamically, library functions are malloc(), calloc(), realloc() and free() are used.
These functions are defined in the <stdlib.h> header file. The concept of **dynamic memory allocation in c language** *enables the C programmer to allocate memory at runtime*
Before learning above functions, let's understand the difference between static memory allocation and dynamic memory allocation.

static memory allocation	dynamic memory allocation
memory is allocated at compile time.	memory is allocated at run time.
memory can't be increased while executing program.	memory can be increased while executing program.
used in array.	used in linked list.

Now let's have a quick look at the methods used for dynamic memory allocation.

malloc()	allocates single block of requested memory.
calloc()	allocates multiple block of requested memory.
realloc()	reallocates the memory occupied by malloc() or calloc() functions.
free()	frees the dynamically allocated memory.

Characteristics of Dynamic Memory Allocation
1. **Flexibility**:
    - Memory can be allocated and deallocated at runtime, enabling the creation of data structures like linked lists, trees, and graphs that can grow or shrink as needed.
2. **Variable Size**:
    - You can allocate memory for structures or arrays whose sizes may change during the program execution.
3. **Manual Management**:

- Unlike static or automatic memory allocation, dynamic memory requires explicit management by the programmer. You must allocate memory using functions like malloc(), calloc(), or realloc(), and free it using free().
4. **Heap Storage**:
    - Dynamically allocated memory comes from the heap, a region of memory used for dynamic allocation. Unlike stack memory, which is automatically managed and has a limited size, heap memory can grow and shrink as needed.
5. **Potential for Fragmentation**:
    - Frequent allocations and deallocations can lead to memory fragmentation, which may affect performance or lead to memory exhaustion if not managed carefully.
6. **Error Handling**:
    - Functions for dynamic memory allocation may fail (e.g., if there's insufficient memory). It's essential to check the return value of these functions to ensure that memory allocation was successful.

DMA functions
Functions for Dynamic Memory Allocation
1. **malloc(size_t size)**:
    - Allocates a block of memory of specified size (in bytes) and returns a pointer to the beginning of the block.
    - The contents of the allocated memory are uninitialized.

int *arr = (int *)malloc(10 * sizeof(int)); // Allocate memory for 10 integers

2. **calloc(size_t num, size_t size)**:
    - Allocates memory for an array of elements, initializes all bytes to zero, and returns a pointer to the memory.

int *arr = (int *)calloc(10, sizeof(int)); // Allocate memory for 10 integers initialized to 0

3. **realloc(void *ptr, size_t size)**:
    - Resizes a previously allocated memory block. If the new size is larger, it may allocate a new block, copy the existing data, and free the old block.

arr = (int *)realloc(arr, 20 * sizeof(int)); // Resize to hold 20 integers

4. **free(void *ptr)**:

o Deallocates previously allocated memory, returning it to the heap for reuse.

free(arr); // Free the memory allocated to arr

C malloc()
The name "malloc" stands for memory allocation.
The malloc() function reserves a block of memory of the specified number of bytes. And, it returns a pointer of void which can be casted into pointers of any form.
Syntax of malloc()
    ptr = (castType*) malloc(size);
Example
ptr = (float*) malloc(100 * sizeof(float));
The above statement allocates 400 bytes of memory. It's because the size of float is 4 bytes. And, the pointer ptr holds the address of the first byte in the allocated memory.
The expression results in a NULL pointer if the memory cannot be allocated.

C calloc()
The name "calloc" stands for contiguous allocation. The malloc() function allocates memory and leaves the memory uninitialized, whereas the calloc() function allocates memory and initializes all bits to zero.
Syntax of calloc()
    ptr = (castType*)calloc(n, size);
Example:
ptr = (float*) calloc(25, sizeof(float));
The above statement allocates contiguous space in memory for 25 elements of type float.

C free()
Dynamically allocated memory created with either calloc() or malloc() doesn't get freed on their own. You must explicitly use free() to release the space.
Syntax of free()
    free(ptr);
This statement frees the space allocated in the memory pointed by ptr.

Example 1: malloc() and free()

```c
// Program to calculate the sum of n numbers entered by the user

#include <stdio.h>
#include <stdlib.h>

int main() {
  int n, i, *ptr, sum = 0;

  printf("Enter number of elements: ");
  scanf("%d", &n);

  ptr = (int*) malloc(n * sizeof(int));

  // if memory cannot be allocated
  if(ptr == NULL) {
    printf("Error! memory not allocated.");
    exit(0);
  }

  printf("Enter elements: ");
  for(i = 0; i < n; ++i) {
    scanf("%d", ptr + i);
    sum += *(ptr + i);
  }

  printf("Sum = %d", sum);

  // deallocating the memory
  free(ptr);

  return 0;
}
```
Output
Enter number of elements: 3
Enter elements: 100
20
36
Sum = 156
Here, we have dynamically allocated the memory for n number of int.

Example 2: calloc() and free()
// Program to calculate the sum of n numbers entered by the user

```
#include <stdio.h>
#include <stdlib.h>

int main() {
  int n, i, *ptr, sum = 0;
  printf("Enter number of elements: ");
  scanf("%d", &n);

  ptr = (int*) calloc(n, sizeof(int));
  if(ptr == NULL) {
    printf("Error! memory not allocated.");
    exit(0);
  }

  printf("Enter elements: ");
  for(i = 0; i < n; ++i) {
    scanf("%d", ptr + i);
    sum += *(ptr + i);
  }

  printf("Sum = %d", sum);
  free(ptr);
  return 0;
}
```
Output
Enter number of elements: 3
Enter elements: 100
20
36
Sum = 156

C realloc()
If the dynamically allocated memory is insufficient or more than required, you can change the size of previously allocated memory using the realloc() function.

Syntax of realloc()
      ptr = realloc(ptr, x);
Here, ptr is reallocated with a new size x.

Example 3: realloc()
```
#include <stdio.h>
#include <stdlib.h>

int main() {
 int *ptr, i , n1, n2;
 printf("Enter size: ");
 scanf("%d", &n1);

 ptr = (int*) malloc(n1 * sizeof(int));

 printf("Addresses of previously allocated memory:\n");
 for(i = 0; i < n1; ++i)
   printf("%pc\n",ptr + i);

 printf("\nEnter the new size: ");
 scanf("%d", &n2);

 // rellocating the memory
 ptr = realloc(ptr, n2 * sizeof(int));

 printf("Addresses of newly allocated memory:\n");
 for(i = 0; i < n2; ++i)
   printf("%pc\n", ptr + i);

 free(ptr);

 return 0;
}
```
Output
Enter size: 2
Addresses of previously allocated memory:
26855472
26855476

Enter the new size: 4
Addresses of newly allocated memory:
26855472
26855476
26855480
26855484

Example Program
Here's an example demonstrating dynamic memory allocation:
```
#include <stdio.h>
#include <stdlib.h>

int main() {
    int n;

    printf("Enter the number of elements: ");
    scanf("%d", &n);

    // Dynamic allocation of memory for n integers
    int *arr = (int *)malloc(n * sizeof(int));

    // Check if memory allocation was successful
    if (arr == NULL) {
        printf("Memory allocation failed!\n");
        return 1; // Exit if allocation failed
    }

    // Initialize and print the array
    for (int i = 0; i < n; i++) {
        arr[i] = i + 1; // Assign values
    }

    printf("Array elements: ");
    for (int i = 0; i < n; i++) {
        printf("%d ", arr[i]); // Print values
    }
    printf("\n");

    // Free the allocated memory
```

```
    free(arr);

    return 0;
}
```
Output Example
If you enter 5 when prompted, the output will be:
mathematica
Copy code
Enter the number of elements: 5
Array elements: 1 2 3 4 5

Summary
Dynamic memory allocation in C provides significant flexibility in managing memory, enabling the creation of complex data structures that can change size during program execution. However, it requires careful management to avoid memory leaks and fragmentation. Always check the success of memory allocations and ensure that you free any dynamically allocated memory when it's no longer needed.

CHAPTER 10: PREPROCESSORS AND MACROS

10.1 Proprocessors Introduction

The source code is the code which is written in a text editor and the source code file is given an extension ".c". This source code is first passed to the preprocessor, and then the preprocessor expands this code. After expanding the code, the expanded code is passed to the compiler.

C macros provide a potent method for code reuse and simplification. They let programmers construct *symbolic names* or phrases that are changed to certain values before the compilation process begins. The use of more *macros* makes code easier to *comprehend, maintain*, and makes mistakes less likely. In this article, we'll delve deeper into the concept of C macros and cover their advantages, ideal usage scenarios, and potential hazards.

In C, a preprocessor is a tool that processes your source code before it's compiled. The C preprocessor is a macro preprocessor (allows you to define macros) that transforms your program before it is compiled. These transformations can be the inclusion of header files, macro expansions, etc. All preprocessing directives begin with a # symbol. For example,
#define PI 3.14

Advantages of Using Macros:

There are various advantages of Macros in C. Some main advantages of C macros are as follows:

Code reuse: By allowing developers to declare a piece of code just once and use it several times, **macros** help to promote modular programming and minimize code duplication.

Code abbreviation: Macros make it possible to **write clear, expressive code** that is simpler to read and comprehend the intentions of the programmer.

Performance Optimization: By minimizing *function call overhead*, macros may be utilized to *optimize code execution*. For instance, it is possible to inline brief pieces of code using function-like macros.

Using **macros, conditional compilation** enables distinct sections of the code to be *included* or *removed* based on *predetermined* circumstances. *Debugging* or *platform-specific code* both benefit from this functionality.

When Using Macros, Exercise Caution:

Use *caution* while constructing function-like **macros** in brackets. Always use brackets to contain *parameters* and the full **macro body** to avoid unexpected outcomes brought on by operator precedence.

Macro Side consequences: *Steer clear* of macros with **negative consequences**. *Multiple evaluations* of macro arguments may result in surprising results since macros are directly substituted.

Use capital letters to distinguish macro names from standard C identifiers and to make the code easier to understand.

10.2 Types of C Preprocessors
List of preprocessor directives in C
The following table lists all the preprocessor directives in C:

Preprocessor Directives	Description
#define	Used to define a macro
#undef	Used to undefine a macro
#include	Used to include a file in the source code program
#ifdef	Used to include a section of code if a certain macro is defined by #define
#ifndef	Used to include a section of code if a certain macro is not defined by #define
#if	Check for the specified condition
#else	Alternate code that executes when #if fails
#elif	Combines else and if for another condition check
#endif	Used to mark the end of #if, #ifdef, and #ifndef

These preprocessors can be classified based on the type of function they perform.
Categories of C Preprocessors
There are 4 Main Types of Preprocessor Directives:
1. Macros

#define,#undef
2. File Inclusion
   # Include
3. Conditional Compilation
   #ifdef, #ifndef, #if, #else, #elif, #endif
4. Other directives
   #line, #error, #pragma

10.2.1 Macros
A macro is a fragment of code that is given a name. In C, Macros are pieces of code in a program that is given some name. Whenever this name is encountered by the compiler, the compiler replaces the name with the actual piece of code. You can define a macro in C using the #define preprocessor directive.
Syntax:
#define *token value*
A macro is a segment of code which is replaced by the value of macro. Macro is defined by #define directive. There are two types of macros:
   1. **Object-like Macros**
   2. **Function-like Macros**

Object-like Macros
Example Program
// C Program to illustrate the macro
#include <stdio.h>

// macro definition
#define LIMIT 5

int main()
{
   for (int i = 0; i < LIMIT; i++) {
      printf("%d \n", i);
   }

   return 0;
}
Output:
0
1
2
3
4
Example Program 2:

```c
#include <stdio.h>
#define PI 3.1415

int main()
{
    float radius, area;
    printf("Enter the radius: ");
    scanf("%f", &radius);

    // Notice, the use of PI
    area = PI*radius*radius;

    printf("Area=%.2f",area);
    return 0;
}
```
Output:
Enter the radius:5.5
Area=77.43

Function like Macros

We can also pass arguments to macros. Macros defined with arguments work similarly to functions.
Examples:
#define MIN(a,b) ((a)<(b)?(a):(b))
#define foo(a, b) a + b
#define func(r) r * r
#define circleArea(r) (3.1415*(r)*(r))

Example Program 1:
// C Program to illustrate function like macros
#include <stdio.h>

// macro with parameter
#define AREA(l, b) (l * b)

int main()
{
    int l1 = 10, l2 = 5, area;

    area = AREA(l1, l2);

    printf("Area of rectangle is: %d", area);

    return 0;

}
Output:
Area of rectangle is: 50

Example Program 2:
```
#include <stdio.h>
#define PI 3.1415
#define circleArea(r) (PI*r*r)

int main() {
   float radius, area;

   printf("Enter the radius: ");
   scanf("%f", &radius);
   area = circleArea(radius);
   printf("Area = %.2f", area);

   return 0;
}
```

10.2.2 File Include Directive

File inclusion preprocessor directives in C allow you to include the contents of one file into another during the preprocessing phase of compilation. This is essential for code organization and reuse, especially when working with large projects. The two primary directives for file inclusion are #include <file> and #include "file".
    For example, #include <stdio.h>
Here, stdio.h is a header file. The #include preprocessor directive replaces the above line with the contents of stdio.h header file.
That's the reason why you need to use #include <stdio.h> before you can use functions like scanf() and printf().
You can also create your own header file containing function declaration and include it in your program using this preprocessor directive.
#include "my_header.h"
    #include <file>
This syntax is used to include standard library headers or system headers. The compiler searches for these files in the system's standard directories.
Example:
#include <stdio.h> // Includes the standard input/output library

int main() {

```
    printf("Hello, World!\n");
    return 0;
}
```
2. #include "file"
This syntax is used to include user-defined header files. The compiler first searches for the file in the directory of the source file and then in the standard directories if it does not find it.

Example: Assuming you have a custom header file named my_functions.h:

my_functions.h:
```
#ifndef MY_FUNCTIONS_H
#define MY_FUNCTIONS_H

void greet(const char* name);

#endif // MY_FUNCTIONS_H
```
my_functions.c:
```
#include "my_functions.h"
#include <stdio.h>

void greet(const char* name) {
    printf("Hello, %s!\n", name);
}
```
main.c:
```
#include <stdio.h>
#include "my_functions.h"  // Including the custom header

int main() {
    greet("Alice");  // Calling the function defined in my_functions.h
    return 0;
}
```
How It Works
1. **Inclusion of Header Files**: The #include directive tells the preprocessor to take the contents of the specified file and insert it into the source code at that location. This is useful for including function prototypes, constants, and other declarations that are used across multiple source files.
2. **Avoiding Multiple Inclusions**: To prevent errors caused by including the same header file multiple times, include guards are

commonly used, as seen in my_functions.h. The #ifndef, #define, and #endif directives ensure that the header's contents are only included once.

Example with Multiple Files

Here's a complete example with multiple files to illustrate how file inclusion works.

File Structure:
```
/project
    ├── main.c
    ├── my_functions.h
    └── my_functions.c
```

my_functions.h:
```
#ifndef MY_FUNCTIONS_H
#define MY_FUNCTIONS_H

void greet(const char* name);
int add(int a, int b);

#endif // MY_FUNCTIONS_H
```

my_functions.c:
```
#include "my_functions.h"
#include <stdio.h>

void greet(const char* name) {
    printf("Hello, %s!\n", name);
}

int add(int a, int b) {
    return a + b;
}
```

main.c:
```
#include <stdio.h>
#include "my_functions.h"

int main() {
    greet("Bob");
    int sum = add(5, 3);
    printf("Sum: %d\n", sum);
    return 0;
```

}
File inclusion directives (#include) are fundamental in C programming for managing code in multiple files. They facilitate modular programming by allowing the separation of declarations and implementations, promoting better organization and maintainability of code. Always use include guards to prevent multiple inclusions and potential conflicts.

10.2.3 Conditional Compilation

Conditional compilation preprocessor directives in C allow you to include or exclude parts of your code based on certain conditions. This is particularly useful for writing code that can compile differently depending on the environment, platform, or specific configuration options. The main conditional compilation directives are #ifdef, #ifndef, #if, #else, #elif, and #endif.

In C programming, you can instruct the preprocessor whether to include a block of code or not. To do so, conditional directives can be used.

It's similar to a if statement with one major difference.

The if statement is tested during the execution time to check whether a block of code should be executed or not whereas, the conditionals are used to include (or skip) a block of code in your program before execution.

Uses of Conditional
- use different code depending on the machine, operating system
- compile the same source file in two different programs
- to exclude certain code from the program but to keep it as a reference for future purposes

Syntax of Conditional Compilation Directives

1. **#ifdef**: Checks if a macro is defined.

```
#ifdef MACRO_NAME
// Code to include if MACRO_NAME is defined
#endif
```

2. **#ifndef**: Checks if a macro is not defined.

```
#ifndef MACRO_NAME
// Code to include if MACRO_NAME is not defined
#endif
```

3. **#if**: Evaluates a constant expression.

```
#if CONDITION
// Code to include if CONDITION is true
#endif
```

4. **#else**: Provides an alternative block of code if the preceding #if, #ifdef, or #ifndef condition is false.

```
#ifdef MACRO_NAME
// Code if MACRO_NAME is defined
```

```
#else
// Code if MACRO_NAME is not defined
#endif
```
    5. **#elif**: Combines #else and #if to provide multiple conditional checks.
```
#if CONDITION1
// Code for CONDITION1
#elif CONDITION2
// Code for CONDITION2
#endif
```
    6. **#endif**: Ends a conditional block started by #if, #ifdef, or #ifndef.
`#endif`

Example Program
Here's an example that demonstrates conditional compilation:
File: main.c:
```
#include <stdio.h>

#define DEBUG  // Comment this line to disable debugging

int main() {
   int x = 10, y = 20;

   #ifdef DEBUG
      printf("Debugging is enabled.\n");
      printf("x = %d, y = %d\n", x, y);
   #endif

   int sum = x + y;
   printf("Sum: %d\n", sum);

   #if defined(DEBUG) && (x < y)
      printf("X is less than Y.\n");
   #else
      printf("X is not less than Y.\n");
   #endif

   return 0;
}
```
Explanation
- If the DEBUG macro is defined (as it is in this example), the debugging information will be printed.
- The program calculates the sum of x and y, and depending on the condition in the #if directive, it will print whether x is less than y.

Outputs

Case 1: With Debugging Enabled (DEBUG is defined)
If you compile and run this program as it is, the output will be:
Debugging is enabled.
x = 10, y = 20
Sum: 30
X is less than Y.

Case 2: With Debugging Disabled (Comment out #define DEBUG)
If you comment out the #define DEBUG line:
// #define DEBUG // Comment this line to disable debugging
Then compile and run the program again, the output will be:
vbnet
Copy code
Sum: 30
X is not less than Y.

Summary
Conditional compilation preprocessor directives provide a powerful way to include or exclude code based on certain conditions, enhancing flexibility and allowing for different behaviors in different environments. This is especially useful for debugging, platform-specific code, or feature toggles. Always remember to end your conditional blocks with #endif to maintain code clarity and correctness.

Exercise Programs

WEEK 1: Basics, Data types
1. Work on Linux Environment to create a C Program
2. Write a C Program to display "Hello World"
3. Write a C Program to display Your name 5 times.
4. Write a C Program to read the values from keyboard and print.
5. Write a C Program to read the value into every data type of C supported and print the values.
6. Write a C Program to read two numbers add them and display their sum.

WEEK 2: Operators
7. Write a C Program to read the radius of a circle, calculate its area and display it.
8. Write a C Program read p, n, r and calculate Simple Interest.
9. For Advanced Learners: Write a C Program to calculate Compound Interest.
10. WACP to calculate the Sum of N natural numbers
11. WACP to calculate Sum of squares of n natural numbers
12. WACP to convert Celsius to Fahrenheit, vice versa conversion
13. WACP to Finding Big and small among two values using ternary operator
14. WACP to Finding Big and small among three values using ternary operator
15. WACP to Finding Big and small among four values using ternary operator

WEEK 3: Operators, Control statements
16. Write a C program to check whether a number is even or odd using if else
17. Write a C program to check whether a number is even or odd using ternary operator (*)
18. Write a C program to check and print whether a user is eligible to vote or not using if else
    Conditions:
    Minimum age required for voting is 18.
    You can use decision making statement.
19. WACP to Swap two values using 3rd variable using ternary operator.
20. WACP to Swap two values without using 3rd variable using ternary operator.

21. Write a C Program to check whether a given year is a leap year or not using ternary operator
22. Write a C program to check whether an alphabet is Vowel or Consonant
    Conditions: Create a character type variable with name of alphabet and take the value from the user. Use Conditional Statements to solve.
23. WACP to Read 6 subjects marks (max 100) of a student and calculate the total, percentage and grade of a student using ternary operator
24. WACP to Read the 6 subjects marks (30 internal, 70 external). Internal marks will be the best of two Mids then calculate the subject wise total, total, percentage and grade of student using Ternary operator

WEEK 4: Control statements, loops
25. WACP to Find Largest and Smallest Number Among Three Number using if else ladder statements
26. WACP to Check a given year is a Leap year or not if else statements.
27. Write a C program to check whether number is positive, negative or zero

Conditions: Create variable with name of number and the value will be taken by user from console. Create this c program code using else if ladder statement.

28. Write a C program to calculate Electricity bill.
Conditions:
    For first 50 units – Rs. 3.50/unit
    For next 100 units – Rs. 4.00/unit
    For next 100 units – Rs. 5.20/unit
    For units above 250 – Rs. 6.50/unit
29. WACP to Read the 6 subjects marks (30 internal, 70 external). Internal marks will be the best of two Mids then calculate the subject wise total, total, percentage and grade of student using if else ladder statements
30. Write a C Program to display 1 to 10 Numbers using while loop.
31. Write a C Program to display even numbers below 20 using do..while loop.
32. Write a C Program to display sum of 20 natural numbers using for loop.
33. WACP to Generate Multiplication Table
34. WACP to Reverse of a Number
35. WACP to calculate all arithmetic operations using switch case.

WEEK 5: loops
36. WACP to check a given values is an Armstrong or not
37. WACP to Check Whether a given Number is a Palindrome or Not
38. WACP to check a given values is a perfect number or not
39. WACP to Print Fibonacci Series using for loop and while
40. WACP to print below pattern

41. WACP to print below pattern

```
1 2 3 4 5
2 2 3 4 5
3 3 3 4 5
4 4 4 4 5
5 5 5 5 5
```

42. WACP to print below pattern

```
1
2 2
3 3 3
4 4 4 4
5 5 5 5 5
```

43. WACP to print below pattern

```
1
1 2
1 2 3
1 2 3 4
1 2 3 4 5
```

44. WACP to print below pattern

```
*
* *
* * *
* * * *
* * * * *
```

44. WACP to print below pattern

```
1 1 1 1 1
2 2 2 2
3 3 3
4 4
5
```

45. WACP to print below pattern

```
5 5 5 5 5
5 5 5 5
5 5 5
5 5
5
```

46. WACP to print below pattern

```
5 5 5 5 5
4 4 4 4
3 3 3
2 2
1
```

47. WACP to print below pattern

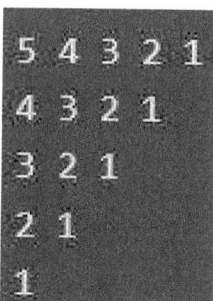
48. WACP to print below pattern

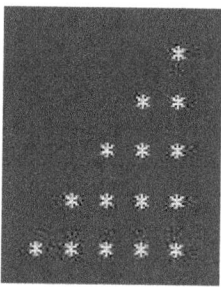
49. WACP to print below pattern

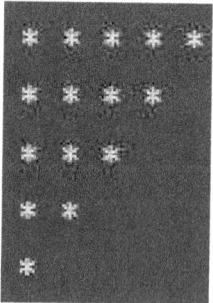
50. WACP to print below pattern

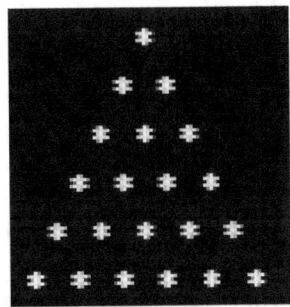

51. WACP to print below pattern

WEEK 6: Functions
52. Write a Function in C Without Arguments and Return Value
53. Write a Function in C Without Arguments and No return Value
54. Write a Function in C With Arguments and no Return Value
55. Write a Function in C With Arguments and return Value
56. Write a C program to find cube of any number using function.
57. Write a C program to find diameter, circumference and area of circle using functions.
58. Write a C program to find maximum and minimum between two numbers using functions.
59. Write a C program to check whether a number is even or odd using functions.
60. Wrie a C program to add two values using call by value.
61. Wrie a C program to add two values using call by reference.
62. Write a Program to swap two integers using a function (call by value).
63. Write a Program to find the maximum of two, three, four, five numbers using a functions
64. Write a C program read an integer from keyboard and find/check the following
    (a)Number is prime or not
    (b)Number is Even or odd

(c)Number Perfect or not
(c)Number Palindrome of not
(d)Number is Armstrong or not   using functions

WEEK 7: Recursion
65. Write a C Program to find the factorial of a given number using recursive function.
66. Write a C Program to print the first 10 Natural Numbers using recursive function.
67. Write a C Program to solve Towers of Hanoi Problem using recursive function.
68. Write a C Program to Find Sum of Digits of a Number using Recursion.
69. Write a C Program to Reverse a Number using Recursion.
70. Write a C Program to Check whether a Number is Prime or Not using Recursion.
71. Write a C Program to Find Product of Two Numbers using Recursion.
72. Write a C Program to calculate the GCD of two numbers using Recursion.

WEEK 8: 1-D Array
73. Write a C Program to take 5 values from the user and store them in an array and display the elements in the array.
74. Write a C program to calculate sum of array elements.
75. Write a C program to calculate the sum, average of an array elements.
76. Write a C Program to read 10 values in an array and display all even numbers in the array.
77. Write a C Program to read 5 floating values in an array and display the sum and average of the element in it.
78. WACP to Find max & min value in an array.
79. WACP to calculate the Sum of even numbers and odd numbers of an array.
80. WACP to implement Array operations
    (a)Insertion at 1st position, last position, kth position
    (b)Deletion at 1st position, kth position, last position
    (c)Updating at 1st position, kth position, last position
    (d)Count no of elements,
    (e)Search elements given element in an array
    (f)Find element at 1st position, kth position, last position
    (g)Forward traversing, Backward/Reverse traversing

WEEK 9: 2-D Array
81. Write a C Program to read elements into a 2 dimensional array and display them.

82. WACP to calculate Sum of all elements of a matrix.
83. Write a C Program to read two matrices and display their sum.
84. WACP to Find the row wise maximum element of array of matrix.
85. WACP to Find the row wise minimum element of array of matrix.
86. WACP to Find the column wise maximum element of array of matrix.
87. WACP to Find the column wise minimum element of array of matrix.
88. Write a C Program to read two matrices and display their product. (Matrix Multiplication).
89. WACP to print the transpose of matrix
90. WACP to calculate the Sum of lower triangular elements of array matrix.
91. WACP to calculate the Sum of upper triangular elements of array matrix.

WEEK 10: Arrays, Strings
92. WACP for Bubble sort techniques.
93. WACP for Selection sort technique.
94. WACP for Linear Search technique.
95. WACP to Find the k-th largest Element of an Array.
96. WACP to Find the k-th smallest Element in an Array.
97. Write a C program to find length of a string.
98. Write a C program to copy one string to another string.
99. Write a C program to concatenate two strings.

WEEK 11: Strings, Pointers
100. Write a C program to check whether a given string is palindrome or not.
101. Write a C program to find total number of alphabets, digits or special character in a string.
102. Write a C program to count total number of vowels and consonants in a string.
103. Write a C Program to swap two strings (Call by Reference)
104. Write a C program to check two strings are equal or not
105. Write a C program to create, initialize and print the value using pointers. (*)
106. Write a C program to add two numbers using pointers.
107. Write a C program to swap two numbers using pointers.
108. Write a C program to swap two arrays using pointers.
109. Write a C program to reverse an array using pointers.

WEEK 12: Structures, Unions
110. Write a C program to store and print the roll no., name, age and marks of a student using structures.

111. Write a C program to store the roll no. (Starting from 1), name and age of 5 students and then print the details of the student with roll no. 2.
112. Create a structure called "Student" with members name, age, and total marks. Write a C program to input data for two students, display their information, and find the average of total marks.
113. Create a structure named Book to store book details like title, author, and price. Write a C program to input details for three books, find the most expensive and the lowest priced books, and display their information.
114. Create a structure named "Employee" to store employee details such as employee ID, name, and salary. Write a program to input data for three employees, find the highest salary employee, and display their information.
115. Write a C program to add, subtract and multiply two complex numbers using structures to function.

WEEK 14: Case Study
116. Write menu driven program to implement the Bank Transactions of customer.
117. Write menu driven program to implement the ATM Transactions of customer at ATM center
118. Write a menu program Student Data base (Reading details, reading marks, calculating to total marks , % and printing, etc).